CAREERS FOR
HEALTH
NUTS
& Others Who
Like to Stay Fit

VGM Careers for You Series

CAREERS
FOR
HEALTH
NUTS
& Others Who
Like to Stay Fit

Blythe Camenson

VGM Career Horizons
a division of *NTC Publishing Group*
Lincolnwood, Illinois USA

Library of Congress Cataloging-in-Publication Data

Camenson, Blythe.
    Careers for health nuts and others who like to stay fit / Blythe Camenson.
        p. cm. --
    Includes bibliographical references.
    ISBN 0-8442-4117-2 (hard). -- ISBN 0-8442-4118-0 (soft)
    1. Allied health personnel--Vocational guidance. I. Title. II. Series.
    R697.A4C35 1995
    610.69--cd20   95-32404
                                                                 CIP

Published by VGM Career Horizons, a division of NTC Publishing Group.
4255 West Touhy Avenue,
Lincolnwood (Chicago), Illinois 60646-1975 , U.S.A.
Manufactured in the United States of America.

6 7 8 9 0 VP 9 8 7 6 5 4 3 2 1

Contents

To Deborah Gordon and Andy Harper,
the nicest health nuts I know

About the Author

A s a full-time writer of career books, Blythe Camenson's main concern is helping job seekers make educated choices. She firmly believes that with enough information readers can find long-term, satisfying careers. To that end, she researches traditional as well as unusual occupations, talking to a variety of professionals about what their jobs are really like. In all of her books she includes firsthand accounts from people who can reveal what to expect in each occupation, the upsides as well as the down.

Camenson's interests range from history and photography to writing novels. She is also director of Fiction Writer's Connection, a membership organization providing support to new and published writers.

Camenson was educated in Boston, earning her bachelor of arts degree in English and psychology from the University of Massachusetts and her master's degree in counseling and education from Northeastern University. She has had several careers herself including: career and educational counselor, psychotherapist, and English as a foreign language teacher.

In addition to *Careers for Health Nuts*, the books she has written for NTC Publishing are *Careers for History Buffs*, *Careers for Plant Lovers*, *Opportunities in Teaching English to Speakers of Other Languages*, *Career Portraits: Travel*, *Career Portraits: Writing*, *Career Portraits: Nursing*, and *Career Portraits: Firefighting*.

Blythe Camenson is also the author of *Working in the Persian Gulf: Survival Secrets for Men and Women* (Desert Diamond Books).

Acknowledgments

The author would like to thank the following health nuts for providing information about their careers:

JOHN BERBERICH — Sports Psychologist
Seattle, Washington

KENT BRINKLEY — Landscape Architect/Garden Historian
Colonial Williamsburg
Williamsburg, Virginia

THERESA BULMER — Store Manager
Cabbages Health Emporium
Delray Beach, Florida

BOBBIE CAMPBELL — Sports Medicine Nurse
Seattle Sports Medicine Clinic
Seattle, Washington

FRANK CASSISA — Certified Personal Trainer
Bally's Scandinavian Health
and Tennis Corporation
Boca Raton, Florida

BEVERLEY CITRON — Assistant Cruise Director
Miami, Florida

HELEN COX — Occupational Therapist
Boca Raton Community Hospital
Boca Raton, Florida

LAURIE DEJONG — Physical Therapist
Boca Raton Community Hospital
Boca Raton, Florida

EMILY FRIEDLAND — Dietitian
Boca Raton Community Hospital
Boca Raton, Florida

STEVE HERRELL — Founder of Steve's Ice Cream
Herrell's Ice Cream
Northampton, Massachusetts

DAVID HIRSCH — Author and Chef
Moosewood Restaurant
Ithaca, New York

LORETTA HODYSS	Extension Agent Cooperative Extension Service West Palm Beach, Florida
RICHARD MATTSON	Professor/Horticultural Therapist Kansas State University Department of Horticulture, Forestry and Recreation Resources Manhattan, Kansas
NANCY MCVICAR	Health Writer *Sun-Sentinel* Fort Lauderdale, Florida
SALLY MILLER	Manager Finger Lakes Organic Growers Cooperative, Inc. Trumansburg, New York
STEPHIE MORIN	Certified Nurse Midwife Cambridge, Massachusetts
BRAD POTTS	Nurse Practitioner Riverside Health Center Cambridge, Massachusetts
REGINA RENTERIA	Counselor, Educator, Director Miami Women's HealthCenter Miami, Florida
NANCY STEVENSON	Horticultural Therapist Cleveland Botanical Garden Cleveland, Ohio
CAROL STULL	Grower Finger Lakes Organic Growers Cooperative, Inc. Trumansburg, New York
ROY UPTON	Herbalist American Herbalist Guild Soquel, California
ROB VERNER	Psychiatric Nurse St. Vincent Charity Hospital Cleveland, Ohio

CHAPTER ONE

Jobs for Health Nuts

H ealth nuts are not, as the term may imply, fanatics (although some individuals may be). Rather, they are people who've made a personal commitment to leading a healthier, more productive lifestyle. Health nuts keep abreast of medical and scientific research and apply the results to their own lives. They've quit smoking and drinking and are careful with any medications they might have to use, often seeking alternative, natural remedies. They pay attention to the food they eat, how it's grown and prepared, avoiding fats and salt and chemical additives. They practice preventative medicine and see their doctors for regular checkups. They know their cholesterol level and keep tabs on their blood pressure. They take care of their bodies with daily exercise, walking or jogging or playing tennis.

But many health nuts worry about more than their own bodies and lifestyles; their concern goes beyond their own backyards to the complex world in which we all live. They fear for the environment and how we are rapidly destroying it. They try to do their part—conserving water, carpooling or bicycling to work, and recycling newspapers, plastic, aluminum cans, and glass.

Even more committed are those who strive to combine their love of and concern for good health and the environment into meaningful work and careers. If you are reading this book, you probably see yourself in that last category. You are someone searching for a way to share what you have learned, a way to give back to the earth that supports you.

Assessing the Options

There are many career options for health nuts, some obvious, some not so. The jobs we'll examine in this book might spark your interest or, with a little creative brainstorming, lead you to other related professions. The real people you'll meet within these pages will give you firsthand insights into what it's like working in the various categories of this rewarding field. By contacting the resources listed in the appendixes you can find even more in-depth information to help with your decision.

But first, let's begin with a little self-assessment. Ask yourself these basic questions:

1. How much time am I willing to invest for education and specialized training?

___ No formalized training (I can use what I already know)

___ Two to three months of on-the-job training

___ One to two years in a technical or associate's degree program

___ Four years in a bachelor's degree program

___ One to five years above the bachelor's in a master's or doctorate program

2. What kind of work setting would I prefer?

___ Outdoors

___ In an office

___ In a hospital or clinic

___ In a restaurant

___ In a gym or health club

___ In a retail store

___ In my own home office

___ Other _____

3. Would I rather work for

___ the government,

___ a private corporation or business,

___ a not-for-profit agency,

or would I rather be

___ self-employed?

4. Do I prefer to work alone or be part of a team?

5. Do I prefer to work with

___ people (___ well people or ___ sick people),

___ food (___ growing ___ preparing ___ selling), or

___ the environment?

6. Do I have good oral and written communication skills?

7. Do I have a love of science and technology?

8. Do I prefer to

___ study and do research,

___ teach, or

___ do hands-on work?

9. Am I willing to relocate?

10. Is salary an important consideration?

After you've answered these questions you have to analyze what your responses imply. A willingness to relocate means that job options are limitless; a desire to stay in one particular area will narrow the opportunities.

Someone with a mistrust of science and technology but with good verbal and communication skills would do well as a writer or educator, not so well as a medical doctor or forest technician.

A team player would fare better in a corporate or government setting than someone who prefers to work alone.

For the more lucrative professions, a desire for an attractive salary would have to be coupled with a willingness to spend several years studying.

Once you have a good idea of who you are and your ideal working conditions, you are ready to take a closer look at some of your career options.

The Right Career for You

What follows is a breakdown of the career categories that would appeal to health nuts. You can read more about the different job titles in the chapters ahead.

Healers and Caregivers

Healers and caregivers are nurturers by nature. They are concerned with both the physical and emotional well-being of the people with whom they work.

Some health nuts prefer working with well people; others derive great satisfaction from helping the sick. They work in traditional medical careers or in some not so traditional. They spend years studying medicine or nursing, or act as counselors, educators, or group facilitators, addressing the many needs of individuals or entire communities.

Work settings are as varied as the careers. Nurturers find employment in hospitals and health clinics, in colleges or child-birth clinics.

Here is a sampling of job titles for health nuts working as nurturers:

Nurse Midwives

Nurse Practitioners

Sports Medicine Specialists

Sports Psychologists

Mental Health Counselors

Healing with Plants

Some health nuts train in alternative approaches, working with herbs or horticulture. They use plants to heal, to teach, and to raise the self-esteem levels of their clients. They find work in private practice or at hospitals, laboratories, or botanical gardens.

Here is a sampling of job titles for health nuts working with the healing properties of plants:

Herbalists

Herbologists

Naturopaths

Pharmacognacists

Horticultural Therapists

Let's Get Physical

Many health nuts who are concerned with physical fitness find satisfying work helping others reach personal goals. They work in private health clubs, spas, gyms, country clubs, civic centers, or YMCAs. And while most careers in fitness deal with well people, some health nuts prefer working with a physically challenged population, providing rehabilitation therapy. These professionals work in hospitals, clinics, or nursing homes.

Here is a sampling of job titles for health nuts concerned with fitness:

Personal Trainers

Fitness Instructors

Athletics Coaches

Physical Therapists

Occupational Therapists

Recreational Therapists

The World of Food

Health nuts are well aware of the importance of food to a long and healthy life. They prefer vegetables that are organically grown without harmful pesticides and chemical fertilizers. Some avoid eating red meat; still others are dedicated vegetarians or vegans.

The world of food offers many career options for health nuts. Some find work on small organic farms or with retail food co-ops. Others gravitate toward natural food stores and restaurants. Still others share information with the public, teaching about good nutrition, weight loss, or diet.

Here is a sampling of job titles for health nuts working in the world of food:

Organic Growers

Organic Farm Managers

Cooperative Extension Service Agents

Natural Food Store Sales

Vegetarian Restaurant Chefs and Servers

Dietitians and Nutritionists

Health and Food Inspectors

The Health Beat—Writing and Reporting on Health Issues

Health and medical issues are of concern to the general public, and most newspapers and many magazines devote space to reports on new developments or trends in the related fields. There are even magazines focused entirely on fitness and lifestyle, and bookstore and library shelves are crammed with books on spiritual and physical wellness. More often than not, self-help and "how-to" books end up cornering slots on the bestseller list.

Health nuts with good writing skills and a little market savvy can learn how to be a part of this health beat, researching and writing articles and health guides.

Here is a sampling of job titles for health nuts with writing skills:

Book Authors

Freelancer Writers

Reporters/Staff Writers

Columnists

Investigative Reporters

Lecturers

Photographers

Healing the Environment

Some health nuts prefer to work with a more global picture; in other words, these are people who can see the forest through the trees. A healthy body and lifestyle is not enough if the environment we live in is not healthy, too.

Those with environmental concerns can find satisfying careers dealing with landscape preservation, environment conservation, wildlife protection, or pollution control.

Although much of it does, not all conservation work takes place out of doors. Drafting tables and computers are as much a part of the field as fire lines and surveying equipment.

Here is a sampling of job titles for health nuts concerned with the environment:

Landscape Architects and Designers

Land Planners

Conservationists

Foresters

Forest Technicians

Park Rangers

Environmental Engineers

Dream Jobs for Health Nuts

Job-hunting health nuts dream of finding a position where their skills and interests can be combined. Would any of these help wanted ads send you racing to the post office to mail off your resume?

Assistant Chef. Collectively run vegetarian eating establishment seeks individual with at least one year's experience working with specialized menus. Some food serving experience is also desired. Duties include planning meals, ordering produce, and assisting in all phases of food preparation. Basic salary plus profit sharing after one year.

Food Co-op Manager. Candidate must be experienced in all phases of food retailing with a minimum of five years in a cooperative setting. Duties include supervising paid staff and volunteers, public relations, budgeting and finance.

Sports Clinic needs experienced sports medicine RN for patient assessment and care. Some on-site work at local sporting events. Good PR skills necessary.

Veteran's Hospital seeks Horticultural Therapist in year-round program. Work with disabled veterans in on-grounds vegetable and flower garden. Knowledge of special access landscaping—raised garden beds, wheelchair ramps—essential.

Experienced Therapist wanted for women's health center. Run support groups, provide individual counseling, and act as a liaison with community organizations. Master's degree in counseling, nursing, or related field required.

YMCA Summer Day Camp needs full-time Water Safety Instructor. Duties include swimming and boating instruction. Some lifeguarding. YMCA or Red Cross certification required.

This is just a small sampling of the work that health nuts can find. In the chapters ahead you will be introduced to many more possibilities.

Salaries for Health Nuts

Salaries vary widely depending on the field you have chosen to enter. Medical doctors are known for the large salaries they earn, but their investment in time and money to become M.D.'s is equally large. Some categories of R.N.'s pay salaries almost equal to a doctor's, while other health nuts might work for an hourly wage.

The region in which you work will also determine salaries. The northeast and west coast typically pay higher wages than other parts of the country, but the cost of living is higher, too.

Self-employed health nuts—free-lance writers or personal trainers, for example—can put in as much time as they choose, determining their own income.

No matter the salary, most health nuts report that working in a field they love more than offsets any income considerations.

The Job Outlook

Interest in health and environment issues has been on the increase in the last two decades or so. More and more people are becoming aware of the need for healthy living in a healthy environment. This awareness has reached to top levels of our government, resulting in legislation for health care and environmental reform. As more and more programs are instituted, more and more jobs will become available.

For those of you still in high school or college, now is a good time to decide what field interests you and pay attention to what the up-and-coming occupations are. Investigating the various options, studying the appropriate courses, and participating in related hands-on internships will prepare you for the plum jobs looming ahead.

Career changers can keep on top of new policies and programs and ready themselves in much the same way. Everyone's job outlook is enhanced by a combination of making educated choices and receiving the right kind of training and experience.

CHAPTER TWO

Jobs for Healers and Caregivers

Nothing is more important to some health nuts than to help others achieve and maintain good health. Health nuts who are healers and caregivers treat their patients holistically, focusing on all aspects of a person's well-being. They view the body as a whole and do not separate physical components from emotional or spiritual ones.

The occupations covered in this chapter are filled with professionals who look at their patients as being basically well. This differs from professionals who adhere to a medical model, which tends to categorize patients as being basically sick. Although some medical doctors, for example, might very well be health nuts, for the most part their training and approach to patient care do not fit the overall theme of this book. Because of this, our focus will be on careers other than traditional medicine.

There are always exceptions, however, and a few categories within the traditional nursing profession will be covered here.

Nurses As Health Nuts

To choose a career in nursing means you have a special gift. You sincerely care about people and you know how to show those feelings. Nurses love working with people, all kinds of people. Your patients might be rich or poor, young or old, from a variety of backgrounds and cultures.

As a nurse you have a lot of different options open to you. In a traditional hospital setting you can work with newborn infants and children, in the emergency room, or in the intensive care unit. You can assist at a birth or during an operation or provide counseling for psychiatric patients.

You can also work in a private counseling center or in an elementary school or university infirmary. Some nurses choose to work in their patients' homes or for a sports clinic, or aboard a cruise ship, or at a summer camp. Other nurses work in nursing homes or even in prisons.

Nurses can also be administrators and educators, directing the care given in a hospital department or teaching future nurses the skills they'll need in this rewarding career.

The nursing categories we will examine here cover sports medicine, nurse midwifery, family practice nursing, and mental health counseling.

Training for Nurses

At present, there are four different ways you can become a registered nurse, or R.N.:

1. Through a two-year community college, earning an associate's degree in nursing;

2. Through a three-year hospital-based nursing school, earning a diploma:

3. Through a four-year university program, resulting in the Bachelor of Science degree in nursing, or the B.S.N., as it is commonly called;

4. And, for those who already have a bachelor's degree in a different subject, there is a "generic" master's degree in nursing, a two- to three-year program beyond the bachelor's degree.

These days, and certainly in the future, the B.S.N. is being considered the minimum qualification for a satisfying career. The two-year associate's degree and the three-year hospital-based diploma programs are very quickly closing down throughout the country and student nurses are being encouraged to enroll in four-year universities.

For many nursing specialties, it is also essential to earn a master's degree or an advanced certificate; and for some nurses, those who wish to teach, for example, a Ph.D. in nursing is required.

After your schooling, you will be expected to take a licensing exam for the basic R.N. and for any of the various specialty areas you might choose.

Nurses in Family Practice

Nurses who choose to work with families have several different options they can follow. They can have their own private practice, just as a doctor does, or they can work as part of a team in hospitals and clinics. Jobs are available in large cities or rural villages—in fact, nurses working with families can find employment almost anywhere. Their patients range from pregnant women and newborn infants to fathers and grandparents and everyone who comes in between.

The two careers this section focuses on—nurse midwife and nurse practitioner—provide a high degree of professional independence as well as personal satisfaction.

The Duties of Nurse Midwives and Nurse Practitioners

Nurse midwives approach pregnancy as a normal condition. They emphasize counseling and information and support, and they have more time to spend with their patients than physicians usually do. A midwife is there with the patient throughout labor, while many physicians are able to attend only the actual birth.

But midwives are trained to recognize complications, and if any should occur, an obstetrician—the physician who is trained to handle these abnormal situations—is consulted, and they work together to ensure the patient's well-being.

The nurse practitioner profession was originally designed more than thirty years ago to provide health care to those who didn't have access to physicians. And in some settings today, in rural villages, for example, nurse practitioners are still the only providers. They are legally licensed to prescribe medication in most states and fully trained to fill in for pediatricians, obstetricians, and general practice physicians. In urban areas, practitioners work with physicians, providing a comprehensive health care package.

Practitioners focus their attention on a patient's common problems, freeing up time for the physician to correct serious ailments. Nurse practitioners are not as disease-oriented; they try to prevent diseases, and, if a disease is not readily correctable, they teach patients how to live with it.

Job Settings for Nurse Midwives and Nurse Practitioners

Nurse midwives and nurse practitioners find work in city hospitals, clinics, and private doctors' offices; in rural areas, such as on Indian reservations, in Alaska, or in the Appalachian Mountains; or around the world with the armed forces or the Foreign Service.

They can also, in much the same way a doctor does, set up their own office and work in private practice. Some nurse midwives and nurse practitioners even make home visits.

Salaries for Nurse Midwives and Nurse Practitioners

Because there is a great demand for nurse midwives and nurse practitioners, salaries are very high, if not the highest in the nursing profession. In fact, a midwife or practitioner can go into private practice and make about the same salary as a doctor with a general practice. This can run to six figures but, of course, depends on the area of the country in which you live and how much competition there is.

Nurse midwives or practitioners who join the armed forces start out at a high military rank and receive all the accompanying benefits. Large private companies, such as in the oil or computer industries with 1,000 or more employees, prefer to hire midwives and practitioners rather than M.D.'s. They can afford to pay attractive salaries, but they still save money.

As one certified nurse midwife put it, "What could be more rewarding than job satisfaction and good money?"

The Job Outlook

The job outlook for nurse midwives and nurse practitioners is excellent. With all of the health care reform being planned, eventually physicians won't make as much money performing normal, routine duties. Their duties will be left to surgery and other complicated procedures and the skills of midwives and practitioners will be utilized more. In essence, costs will be kept down and everyone will save money.

But cost is not the only factor ensuring a good job outlook. There are many regions in the country that don't attract enough physicians. There are also some patient populations, such as the elderly or inner city teens, that are being neglected. Midwives and practitioners are in even more demand to fill in in these areas.

Stephie Morin, Certified Nurse Midwife

Stephie has been a certified nurse midwife (R.N., C.N.M.) since 1986. She works in a hospital and clinic in Cambridge, Massachusetts.

Stephie talks about her job, how she got started and what her duties are. "When I was just out of high school I met a nurse who was going to become a nurse midwife, and that was the first I had heard of the career. At the same time, a woman I knew was going to have a baby and I got to be at the birth. It just clicked and I knew that's what I wanted to do.

"A nurse midwife is trained in all areas of normal obstetrics, well-woman gynecological care, care of the newborn, and care of normal healthy women throughout their childbearing cycle, and afterward, too. In the United States, most midwives work in hospitals, but some work in birthing centers and some do home care.

"I work with a group of other midwives; our midwifery service is employed by the hospital and we also work with a group of physicians. Occasionally I travel to various community-based health centers, but all the births I attend are in the hospital.

"A woman comes in for prenatal care at the health center. She'll see me for her first visit, which I hope will be early on in her pregnancy. I'll take a health history and I'll spend time getting to know her, giving her information about our service, about her pregnancy. I'll do some blood work, a physical exam, decide if any tests are needed, make any referrals—to a nutritionist, for example, or sometimes to a social worker—then I'll set up her next visit with me.

"During follow-up appointments we talk about how she's feeling, if the baby's moving yet—and we always listen to the baby's heart and measure the belly to see how it's growing.

"When my patient goes into labor, either I or one of my co-workers will meet her at the hospital. We'll evaluate her baby and her labor with different monitoring devices. We support her through the different stages of labor—a nurse will be there, too, and a doctor is always available in case of complications. And if the woman wants any medication, we're able to give it to her.

"After the baby is born, we have follow-up visits to teach her about newborn care and what to expect from her body as she recovers from the delivery.

"Delivering a baby can be a difficult time and the women appreciate the help you give them. You get really close to your patients; some come back for their second babies and you become almost a part of their family. I've even had quite a few women name their babies after me. They send pictures and you get to see how your namesake grows up.

"But people have their babies all times of the day and night and on weekends. It's hard if you have to work in the middle of the night—you lose sleep sometimes and you put in long hours. But the rewards more than make up for it. It's a great honor to take care of women during such an important time in their lives and to see them go from the early stages of pregnancy to becoming mothers.

"I remember the first delivery I attended when I was eighteen years old. It was at the birth of my friend's baby and it was the one event that made me decide to become a midwife.

"My friend wanted to have a more natural delivery than was common at that time. She wanted the baby to have a Leboyer bath, she wanted her friends there in addition to the baby's father, and she wanted someone there to take pictures. I was invited because she knew I was interested in health care and I had been friends with her during her pregnancy.

"I stood at the foot of the bed with another friend of hers, who passed out. (She started speaking French, even though she was an American, and then she hit the floor.) There was meditational-style music playing and just natural light—no bright, artificial lights. The actual birth really blew me away. I was profoundly moved. Looking back I realized that I wasn't moved toward wanting to have a baby (even though I have one now), but more toward being the person who helped other people have babies.

"I was amazed at the power of birth. I remember thinking it was incredible that there had been six people in the room, then all of a sudden there were seven. But no one had walked in the door.

"It changed my life."

Brad Potts, Nurse Practitioner

Brad Potts experimented with a lot of different careers—oceanography, respiratory therapy, even auto mechanics—before he discovered nursing. He now has a B.S.N. and an M.S. degree in primary care. He works at Riverside Health Center in Cambridge, Massachusetts, and loves being able to be involved with the whole family and to focus on people who are in good health.

Brad talks about his job: "A nurse practitioner evaluates a patient's total health care needs. My patients are anywhere from two weeks old to elderly. Initially, we do a head-to-toe physical and a complete health assessment. If a patient comes in with a specific complaint that's complicated and would require complicated intervention, we can refer him or her to a physician, or if it's a common health problem, we can handle it ourselves.

"I really like being able to take care of the whole family— the newborns, mom and dad, grandmom and granddad, and aunts and uncles and sisters and brothers—because health care is more than just the individual. Where you come from, the culture you're in, the beliefs of your parents or grandparents— it's all a big influence. If one person is sick, it affects everybody. When I know what's going on in the family, it helps me deal with all the family members. If a baby is sick, for example, and I'm seeing Grandmother, I know she might be very upset about the baby and might not be sleeping well.

"But there are always too many people to see and not enough time to spend with them, so you can feel pulled from all directions. It's a universal problem. So many people need health care and there are just not enough people and not enough time to take care of everyone the way you'd like.

"And the paperwork is terrible. You have to document everything. You worry about medical/legal issues. You don't want to end up in court. I have malpractice insurance through my job, but I also carry an additional policy for more protection. These days, everyone seems to be lawsuit-happy and anyone who had any contact, even if they just said 'hello,' could be named in the lawsuit. It's gotten out of hand.

"And being a nurse, who also happens to be a man, can cause some awkward moments. An obstacle that I'm always trying to overcome is that I'm not a male nurse, I'm a nurse practitioner and I see all patients—men and women.

"In nursing school I was always assigned to male patients. I used to have to ask to get a female patient assignment. My being there was awkward for my instructors, who were all women; they didn't know how to deal with it.

"Sometimes, because I'm a male, patients assume I must be a doctor. I'm always correcting that impression—I think it's important that people understand the difference between doctors and nurses. But I'm more likely to run into discrimination by my colleagues—female nurses—than by my patients.

"A male will come in with a sore throat, for example, and a female colleague will assign him to me. If a female came in with a sore throat, she'd be referred to the other nurse practitioner I work with, a female.

"I've had to go out to the people who schedule the appointments and instruct them not to steer female patients to female providers and male patients to the males. I talk to my colleagues on a regular basis about this. Initially, I had to do it every day. It's better now, but I still have to address the problem at least once a month.

"The advantage I do see to being a man who is a nurse is that I can be a role model for young men. Oftentimes, a male might think that nursing would be something he'd like to do, but because it's not what men usually do, he might shy away. At least they can see me out there, a typical man, who's doing nursing as his chosen career."

Is This the Right Career for You?

Ask yourself these questions to assess if you have what it takes to make a good midwife or nurse practitioner:

Am I good with my hands?

Do I enjoy studying science?

Am I able to keep track of my activities in writing? (Do I keep a journal or diary, for example?)

Can people read my handwriting?

Am I willing to learn another language?

Am I a good listener?

Am I interested in helping people?

Can I avoid feeling squeamish at the sight of blood or if someone's in pain?

Can I make a commitment and follow it through?

Am I willing to work hard?

Can I work as part of a team?

Training for Nurse Midwives and Practitioners

There are different ways to become a midwife. Stephie's program at Yale combines an R.N. with midwifery training and a master's degree in nursing. If you're not a nurse when you start the program, it takes three years.

But you don't have to be a nurse to be a midwife. Non-nurse midwives are called lay midwives, or empirical midwives, depending upon the region. There are restrictions in different states, and noncertified nurse midwives may not be licensed to the same degree or even legally recognized—it depends on the state. For more information, contact the College of American Nurse Midwives, listed in Appendix A.

But all nurse midwives and nurse practitioners study in special programs above the R.N. or B.S.N., receiving master's degrees and additional training. They also take licensing exams for their specialties.

Sports Medicine

Sports medicine is a subspeciality of orthopedic medicine and deals primarily with injuries received during athletic activities. Sports medicine doctors are mainly orthopedic surgeons who see patients when it's too late to institute preventative measures. Sports medicine nurses care for patients suffering from strains, sprains, torn ligaments and muscles, fractures, and dislocations. Patients could be Little League shortstops, professional ballet dancers, ice skaters, aerobics exercisers, or marathon runners. Anyone with an active lifestyle can suffer a sports-related injury. It's the job of the sports medicine nurse to take a patient's history, assist the doctor with his or her treatment plan, and educate the patient so future injuries can be avoided.

Sports medicine nurses work in clinics, some hospitals, training rooms, rehabilitation centers, outpatient centers, and school infirmaries. Some nurses also work at first aid stations at the various sporting events. They often function as part of a team with physicians and surgeons and physical therapists. (You can read about careers in physical therapy in Chapter Four.)

Bobbie Campbell, Sports Medicine Nurse

Bobbie works at the Seattle Sports Medicine Clinic, a private enterprise that is owned by a physician and a physical therapist. She has been a sports nurse for close to twenty-five years.

Bobbie talks about her job: "I work about thirty-six hours a week. My hours can vary but they're almost always Monday through Friday. I can arrive at 7 A.M. to a full schedule of patients. I'll escort them to the exam rooms, take histories and do brief screenings. If necessary, I'll take blood pressures and interview them about how they got their injuries. I work with the doctor during patient examinations. I write down everything he says and take notes for the patients. After the doctor leaves the room, I go over everything the doctor told the patients—the diagnosis, the plan for treatment, what they're supposed to do at home. I might give them samples of medication and explain the side effects—there's a lot of explanation to the patients. If needed I might also give an injection or take an X ray.

"You have a lot of patient contact and generally you are dealing with a healthy and well-motivated population. I really like being able to share knowledge and educate people to prevent injuries.

"The hours are pleasurable, too—much better than hospital work. The job is varied; there are a lot of different aspects to it. I work with different age groups and I get to incorporate a lot of the general knowledge I learned in my nursing program. You can take your education and skills and use them often. And you get to go to the ballet and sporting events.

"The only downside I can think of is that most of the patients are in a hurry to get well. They're anxious to get back to their sport, and they want to get back now! That can be a great incentive, but it can also be a pressure. Bodies can heal only so quickly.

"But I love the variety and the challenge of the work. It's never boring."

Some Advice from Bobbie

"First, you should be interested in a healthy lifestyle. And you have to want to work with patients; you're not going to be behind a desk. You have to be able to talk to patients and explain and teach. It's a teamwork approach. You work with the doctor and the physical therapist.

"You should also be able to do more than one thing at a time—it's demanding. You might be working with the patient and then there's a telephone call, and at the same time the doctor is asking you to do something and you have to take an X ray. It can all pile up at once and you have to have communication skills and the ability to delegate.

"Then, make sure you get involved with sports. If you can't participate for some reason, then get involved in athletic training. Get down to the training room and work with the coaches. Learn what the athletes need. Volunteer your time at local sporting events. Be a team manager. This is how you find out if it's for you. I've known kids who really got involved, then went on to become athletic trainers, physical therapists, nurses, and doctors. Take basic anatomy and physiology courses to see if it appeals to you. And definitely get a B.S.N. I would even suggest going on afterward for an advanced nurse practitioner degree. More doors will be open to you. The three-year hospital-based R.N. programs are fewer and fewer."

Training for Sports Medicine Nurses

Sports medicine nurses should have at least an R.N. with a B.S.N. preferred. It's also a good idea to have some specialized training. Several colleges and universities offer degrees in this field; for a list of these institutions, contact the American College of Sports Medicine (ACSM) at the address given in Appendix A. Programs are open to registered nurses, licensed practical nurses, and others. It's also possible to get a master's degree in sports medicine.

Counseling and Psychology

As a counselor, you can choose a variety of settings in which to work and a variety of people to see. You can work in a hospital with acute or chronic psychiatric inpatients, for example, or see clients in a clinic or counseling center on an outpatient basis. The work atmosphere and your duties will vary with the setting.

The World of Mental Health Counseling

A variety of professionals work in the mental health field. Medical doctors can specialize in psychiatry and then, as psychiatrists, work full-time in a hospital or have a private practice with hospital privileges. This means that they are able to admit any of their patients who might need hospital care.

Registered nurses can also opt for a career as counselors or psychiatric nurses, working in hospitals or clinics. Many study for a master's degree above the B.S.N.

Psychologists spend many years in college earning a Ph.D. They work similarly to some psychiatrists, but they leave the prescribing of medications to the M.D.'s.

Psychotherapists, social workers, and family therapists usually have master's degrees and work in hospitals or private practice or for government agencies.

Counselors also work in college and university counseling centers, helping students with personal, academic, and career issues.

As a counselor you can work with very emotionally disturbed patients or with patients who are basically well and just need support working through problems. In order to make the right career choice, it is important to understand the type of work you would be doing. In a hospital setting you would deal with all types of patients. Many of them could be chronically ill without much hope for improvement. They could be severely depressed, suicidal, or violent—not able to function in their normal lives.

Generally, in mental health clinics or health centers, patients—or clients, as they are normally called—will have less severe problems and the opportunities to help and see improvement are greater. You might work with clients going through a divorce or grieving over the loss of a child or a spouse.

What Makes a Good Counselor

Counselors need to possess certain skills. How many can you check off?

___ Good people skills/the ability to interact well with people

___ Ability to be supportive and nurturing

___ Good listening skills

___ Flexible attitude

___ Tolerance toward people you don't understand

___ Well-organized

Your Work Conditions

Work conditions vary depending upon the setting. Hospital nurses often work erratic hours—they can be scheduled for holidays, weekends, nights, evenings, and days. Counselors in a clinic setting generally have the benefit of more traditional hours, Monday through Friday, working only an occasional evening or weekend.

Hospital settings more typically follow a medical model, viewing the people they're helping as "patients" who are sick, relying on medication as a large segment of the therapy process.

Therapists in clinics view the people they are helping as basically well. Therapy is usually more active, relying on talking, support, and education, working toward specific, achievable goals.

Getting a Head Start

If you are in high school or college you can start off by getting involved in any peer counseling programs your school might offer. Later, you can volunteer and then find part-time work in a variety of mental health settings. During this process you will get a feel for what the work is really like and you will be able to make an informed choice. You will also learn how to assess yourself and to see if you have what it takes.

Regina Renteria, Counselor, Educator, and Director of a Women's Health Center

Regina has been a nurse for seventeen years and a counselor/educator at the Miami Women's HealthCenter for five years. She is currently working on her master's degree in clinical psychology and loves being able to offer support and information to her clients.

Regina talks about her clinic and the work she does there: "Our clinic is a department of a small community hospital. We're wellness-oriented in that we deal mainly with a population of well women. We try to meet our client's health information needs and address their emotional well-being. We offer a lot of different support groups. They're basically designed for women because men don't often come to them. We have support groups for women who have had breast cancer. We have all kinds of bereavement groups, such as for widows, or for parents who have lost a child, or for adults who have lost a parent. We also have a weekly domestic violence support and education group for women. By giving them support and information we help empower women.

"We also run workshops on self-esteem, relationship skills, communication skills, assertiveness training, parenting, and adjustment to divorce. Our clients are mostly working and professional women, thirty-five to fifty-five years old.

"In the morning I might have a few one-on-one counseling sessions with clients, covering divorce or self-esteem issues.

"Then there's the administrative duties, the paperwork. And I coordinate with other health care professionals and make referrals for my clients.

"I also sometimes give presentations in the community for a women's organization or a business. Right now I'm working on a workshop for the postal service on managing anger. It's called The Anger in You.

"In the afternoon I attend a meeting or two then work on our newsletter, which we distribute to our clients. I have to read a lot, too. There's always a lot of new information coming into the clinic and I have to keep informed.

"What I like most about my job is getting to work with women who are basically well. Sometimes in a hospital setting you can feel as if your efforts are not showing results, but in this kind of job you can feel you're making a difference. You can see your clients getting their needs met.

"I also like the idea of being independent. In my field you can collaborate with other professionals but you're not given a prescribed way of doing things. I can be very creative.

"In fact, I like everything about my job. I can't think of even one negative."

A Special Event at Regina's Clinic

At least once a year at the Miami Women's HealthCenter they invite famous speakers to talk to the women in the community and to serve as role models. Among the celebrity guests they've hosted are Joan Rivers, Ivana Trump, Stephanie Powers, and Joan Lunden. But the person who impressed Regina the most was super-model Christie Brinkley.

Regina explains: "Christie spoke to us about her life and reflected on her career. She's a vegetarian and an exercise fanatic, but except for a brief period when she tried to slim down like all the other models, she never tried to starve herself. She has a round, wholesome look to her, which was a trend she set. She broke into modeling on the heels of the very skinny models.

"She talked about what you see in the magazines, that it's not real. There's a lot of touching up that goes on, pinning up, pulling back. And girls look at these magazines and see these images and think that the models look like that all the time. It sets an impossible standard for them to follow.

"I also got to know Christie a little bit personally and discovered that she's a real nice lady—very down to earth, with a very sensible outlook. She has a great sense of humor and is able to laugh at herself. I didn't find her to be egotistical; she's really interested in other people. It was a very positive experience and I think she's an excellent role model. I felt really good about meeting her and helping to bring her to the health center."

Sports Psychology

Sports psychology is the application of psychological principles to assist athletes, coaches, and anyone else involved in the pursuit of improved physical performance.

In other countries sports psychology has been utilized to assist world-class athletes for many years, probably going back to the 1930s. In the United States it was developed in the 1970s and 1980s, and now our Olympic contestants as well as other athletes are trained in the use of psychological principles to improve their performance.

John Berberich, Sports Psychologist

John Berberich is a clinical psychologist with a private practice in Seattle, Washington. He uses the principles of sports psychology in helping the many athletes he sees.

John talks about his job: "I see athletes and coaches mainly, sometimes parents who may be having adverse interactions with their children. I've dealt with athletes from grammar school, junior high, high school, college, and professional and Olympic athletes.

"Think about what is involved in athletic performance. You have a system in which you can quickly measure whether somebody is improving, and in general that's not often true in life. You have subjective measures when you have a clinical patient in your office who talks about 'I'm feeling better,' or 'I'm feeling worse.'

"But with athletic performance—speed, time elapsed, heights achieved, number of bull's-eyes, number of tackles, number of block kicks—those kinds of things can be measured. And you're dealing within a circumscribed event that has certain rules and regulations and a limited time period in which it occurs.

"The first thing all of us know is that our level of stress or tension affects performance. So we generally teach athletes to decrease the amount of stress they experience so as to optimize their performance. When you have too much stress you don't do as well as when you have less. But there's a point at which that becomes false. You can have too little stress. You need to be psyched up. But generally we teach the opposite, to psych down. Too much stress can cause choking. 'I couldn't perform in the way I wanted because I was so tense I wasn't able to make the free throw; in fact, I shot it three feet short,' or whatever else it might be.

"We also assist through the use of imagery—that is, your own imagination. You can practice performing successfully in your mind and that does improve performance.

"You also teach principles of good thinking. Here's an example. Vasily Alexiev was a Russian weight lifter and a great one. At one point in his training his coaches told him to do a maneuver with a weight below a weight he had previously been successful with. He complied. They then took him to the scales and showed him that the weight he had lifted was more than a world record and much more than he had ever done before. They tricked him in a very important way, showing him that what he thought had a great effect on what he was capable of doing.

"So you teach people to imagine things that, if they were true, would produce the desired effect. And you increase the probability. If one were to think of a weight as something other than a weight, and someone had to move it to save one's life or to give pleasure or whatever it might be, you could expect that the person would be more likely to do better than he had done before, using that kind of imagery.

"Another example. There is an event called the biathlon. In that event contestants will travel on cross-country skis with a rifle strapped to their back over a long distance of hilly terrain that's very tiring. They are then expected to go immediately to a firing area and shoot the rifle accurately. They are out of breath and they have rapid heartbeat. When you're breathing hard and hold a rifle to your shoulder, your breathing affects your aim because you can't hold the rifle steady. Your heartbeat—if it is, for instance, at 180 beats a minute, which is not uncommon—will cause the barrel of the gun to jiggle. You can't shoot accurately under those circumstances. But we can teach people to reduce their heart rate very rapidly with a single thought.

"It's Pavlovian conditioning, and that thought can be anything. Just as Pavlov's dog learned to salivate at the sound of a bell, so can athletes be trained to relax their heart rate with a cue, a single word, for example. Richard Suinn, who has been an Olympic psychologist for several years, trained the first American athlete to medal in the biathlon to change his heart rate from 180 beats per minute down to 80 in a very short period of time. What he did was pair a word with a relaxed state. When the athlete reached the firing area and said the word to himself, he was able to decrease his heart rate very rapidly. The word was 'rock,' but any word can be used.

"Athletes can image an entire performance and work on their technique. I've worked with many athletes that way, having them imagine their technical skills and being in better control of themselves, and teaching them healthy ways to think in order to decrease their stress.

"There are also the principles of learning and motivation, which you teach to coaches so they use positive as well as negative reinforcement. We teach them to be more sensitive to their players' differing needs. Some young athletes are in the sport for more social reasons, yet they want to improve their skills, and others are completely in it for their competitive, self-aggrandizement kinds of needs, and those people are different and you might motivate them very differently.

"Some athletes have large egos and others can take a whole lot of correction in front of others, so you teach coaches to be sensitive, to pay close attention to what they observe in the athlete."

Sometimes there are reluctant athletes—a Little Leaguer who would be happier reading a good book, for example, but is pushed into the sport by overenthusiastic parents.

"In a situation like that," John says, "you work with the entire family to make sure they appreciate the influence they're having and the unhappiness that's being generated. Generally, the outcome of that is a happy 'I don't want to do this' and the family saying 'Okay, you don't have to.' My goal is to assist people to do what they want to do, not what they're being forced to do."

Getting Started in Sports Psychology

There are no pure sports psychology training programs; most sports psychologists have a Ph.D. or related degree in clinical psychology and study sports psychology as a subspecialty. Some psychologists make sports psychology the focus of their practice; others incorporate the principles and techniques into a general practice.

But getting into a clinical psychology program is very competitive. "There are something like four hundred applications for one opening," John says. "You have to have good grades and do well on your GREs."

The doctoral program is generally four to five years above the bachelor's, and then to be licensed, in most states you would need to pass a written and oral examination and have completed 1,500 hours of post-doctoral supervised training.

John Berberich's Background

John Berberich received his Ph.D. in clinical psychology at UCLA in 1968 and in 1979 added sports patients to his existing practice. He became versed in this specialized field through his own readings and also because he had been a professional basketball player for the San Francisco Saints in the old American Basketball League in 1961 and 1962.

"There's an advantage to having a sports background," John admits, "and to having been a competitor and having played at a relatively high level. I became attracted to the field of sports psychology because it was something new and different. It was emerging when I developed my interest in it and it sounded as if it would be fun. There's an excitement working with extremely motivated people who will do anything to improve their performance. You don't ever have to worry about them coming in and telling you they didn't try the ideas that were generated. And it's easy to observe your results. You're not dealing with seriously emotionally disturbed people, but rather with very intact people generally. It's very gratifying to see people improve. And if you're lucky enough to work with people who represent the United States, in the Olympics or the World Cup, for example, that's a real pleasure.

"But professional athletes can be among the hardest to deal with. They think they've got it all worked out and feel much more stigmatized by seeing a sports psychologist than a high schooler or college player. Olympic players are eager to do anything—their chances come up only once every four years. Sports psychology is very well accepted among Olympic coaches and athletes.

"But keep in mind that if someone wants to have an in-the-office practice, you don't do that with sports psychology. You go to the field, you watch and interact with the players. For many this is a benefit to the profession, but it can also be a downside. You might be spending a considerable amount of time in activities for which you're not being paid."

To get a new sports psychology practice going, John suggests that you let your name be known. Go to the local high schools, give talks, or work with the kids on a gratis basis to begin with. Learn the language of the sport, watch and help and eventually referrals will start coming your way.

Hospital Counseling

In a hospital setting counselors can work with a variety of short-term or long-term patients. Because the medical model often functions vigorously at psychiatric hospitals or on psychiatric units within a general hospital, many health nuts might not find this to be the ideal setting.

Listen to Rob Verner, then decide.

Rob Verner, Psychiatric Nurse

Rob Verner has been a psychiatric nurse for over fifteen years. He works in an inpatient hospital setting and enjoys the one-on-one contact with his patients. Rob finds his work meaningful and satisfying.

"I work on three different units in my hospital. There's a psychiatric emergency room, from where most of our patients are admitted, a short-term acute psychiatric unit for agitated patients, and a unit for adolescents age ten to eighteen.

"Some of our patients are very depressed, even suicidal. Others suffer from schizophrenia and hear voices or see things that aren't there. Some of the patients are violent. I can put on the nightly news before I come into work and hear about how the police apprehended a man waving a gun on the street. I know that when I get to work, he'll be there waiting for me.

"The adolescents we get have severe problems at home or at school or they're depressed or suicidal. Occasionally, we get an early schizophrenic who is starting to hear voices. That's very sad.

"I start my day with the report from the last shift and find out what was happening on the unit while I was off. Then I greet all the patients I am assigned to and tell them who I am and that I'll be taking care of them. I discuss with them any special activities going on, with the recreational therapist or occupational therapist, for example.

"Later in the day I hand out medications, then talk individually with the patients about why they're in the hospital and how they're feeling.

"I also spend a lot of time setting limits and redirecting, trying to control behavior. A lot of the time I find myself saying things like, 'You can't go into that other patient's room; you need to stay in your own room or in the day room; you can't threaten to hit that person because you're angry with them; you have to put that chair down and not hit anybody with it.' It's an acute unit and we have some violent patients.

"I also teach patients about their medications and help them look for alternative ways to deal with their problems. Then there's the administrative duties, charting on the patients or attending meetings with the psychiatrists, social workers, and various therapists to discuss care plans.

"I like having a lot of contact with just a few patients. I could have gone into psychology or even psychiatry if I had wanted to, but I think in those fields you see an awful lot of patients for a brief period of time during the week. What I am attracted to is spending a lot of time with fewer patients.

"But it's very emotionally stressful, the violence and the behavioral problems. And it's hard dealing with other people's problems; you can lose the energy to deal with your own problems.

"The hours can be very difficult, too, when you're rotating shifts, working nights, evenings, working days. You can get confused as to what day it is.

"And sometimes it's stressful dealing with the doctors. You might have different ideas how a patient should be treated and you can spend a lot of time trying to get ahold of the doctor for medication orders, etc. Generally, in psychiatric nursing, you don't get to use your own brain sometimes. You know what the patient needs, but you can't do anything until you get ahold of the physician. Having your actions limited is frustrating.

"It's also frustrating dealing with the chronically ill. You can't cure anybody, can't make the disease go away.

"But there are exceptions to that. I had a patient, a young, very angry high school student, who was having serious difficulties at home—an alcoholic father, brothers who were in trouble with the police, one who had even ended up in prison.

"Before we met, he had started breaking into people's homes. One day he let himself into an apartment and sat down quietly on the couch to wait for the residents to come home. As it turned out, he knew he needed help, but didn't know how to go about getting it. He had figured out that by doing this, maybe someone would help him.

"The police were called and he was taken to jail, but the jail let him come to my hospital to get treatment while they were waiting to decide what to do with him. He's the only kid I went to the courthouse for. He didn't belong in a detention home, he hadn't hurt anyone—he was obviously looking for help.

"The judge let him go and he stayed in the hospital for about two months. I spent a lot of time working with him, talking about the anger he felt at his family. We looked at the ineffective ways his brothers had dealt with their anger and how he needed to be smart and come up with a better plan—unless he wanted to go to prison, because that's where he was heading.

"I learned later through mutual contacts that he finished high school, then went on to college and became a nurse. I was so happy he had done well. Unlike most of the patients I see now, there was real potential for him to turn his life around. Because he had chosen to become a nurse meant to me that perhaps I had helped him, and that he wanted to help other people in the same way. It's a nice feeling thinking I'd had some positive effect on him, that I had done something right.

"The few people you can really help make it all worthwhile."

Test Your Self-Esteem

Counselors regularly work with clients and patients who suffer from low self-esteem, but before these professionals can be really effective, they must have a strong sense of their own self-worth.

How high is your self-esteem? Answer the statements *True* or *False*, then find your rating.

1. I normally feel warm and happy toward myself. ____

2. I normally speak up for my own opinions. ____

3. I normally do my own thinking and make my own decisions. ____

4. I willingly take responsibility for the consequences of my actions. _____

5. I feel free to express love, anger, joy, resentment, and all my other emotions. _____

6. I rarely experience jealousy, envy, or suspicion. _____

7. I don't feel put down or rejected if someone disagrees with me. _____

8. I readily admit my mistakes, shortcomings, and defeats. _____

9. I can make and keep friends without exerting myself. _____

10. Everything doesn't always have to be perfect. _____

11. I accept compliments and gifts without embarrassment. _____

12. I am normally friendly, considerate, and generous with others. _____

Your Self-Esteem Rating

The more questions you were able to answer with *True*, the better your self-esteem. Count your *True* answers, then find your score below.

0 to 4 — You need to work on your self-esteem. Talk to someone you trust about the things that concern you.

5 to 8 — Your self-esteem is not too bad, but there are still areas you could work on. Again, discuss your concerns with a counselor or someone else whose opinion you respect.

9 to 12 — Congratulations! Your self-esteem is excellent. You are confident and mature and you really take care of yourself.

CHAPTER THREE

Healing with Plants

F or thousands of years people have recognized the healing properties of plants. Before the creation of synthetic medicines, ancient cultures were knowledgeable about each plant's function and how to tap into its strengths.

In modern times in the United States, this discipline has become almost a lost art. But not quite. Health nuts around the world still recognize the value of plants for healing.

In addition to their aesthetic value and their life-sustaining importance as food, plants have always been the basis for curing common and not-so-common ailments. Products derived from plants and the act of working with plants in general provide us with therapeutic and curative powers.

Health nuts who also love plants can find rewarding careers in this area.

Herbalism

Old Webster's Dictionary from the 1800s defined an herbalist as one involved with the commerce of plants: an herb doctor or root doctor. Today, most people refer to herbalists as those who use or pick herbs for medicine.

Professional herbalists fall into several different categories.

WILDCRAFTERS pick herbs that are going to be used for medicinal purposes.

FARMERS who specifically grow herbs for medicine are considered to be herbalists.

HERBOLOGISTS, as the suffix implies, are people who study herbs and identify them but don't necessarily use them.

The Birth of an Herbalist

Roy Upton, president of the American Herbalist Guild, is an herbalist who, through his writing and lecturing, is involved with teaching people the medicinal value of plants. He writes books and magazine articles and teaches classes across the country. He also consults with people about their health needs and which types of herbs they can use to deal with different types of ailments. In addition, Roy works full-time for a manufacturer of medicinal products, responsible for quality control and answering customers' questions.

Roy developed his expertise in an interesting manner. He lived for three and a half years on different Native American reservations in Washington, Nevada, and New Mexico learning about herbs and their uses. "I just learned about herbs as a process of living," explains Roy. "People got sick, the medicine people picked herbs and made teas or poultices. I absorbed what I was seeing and started learning."

He then spent four years in St. Thomas, Virgin Islands, and studied the Caribbean's ethnobotany (local cultural use of plants for medicine).

"There are different herb doctors in the Caribbean; people go to them just like they go to regular doctors here. One of my teachers was too old to gather the plants, so I would do it for her, and then she would tell me what they were used for. I would then comb through all the literature in the libraries, and eventually, by working on a project for the local college in St. Thomas, cataloging the different medicinal plants and setting up medicinal herb gardens, I learned even more."

From there Roy traveled to California, where he is currently based, and entered a three-year program studying traditional Chinese medicine.

For those seeking training as herbalists but are unable to follow in Roy's footsteps, there are a number of residency programs in the United States. There are also correspondence courses and various lectures, seminars, and workshops held across the country. The American Herbalist Guild publishes an inexpensive directory which lists all the different programs. It is available by writing to them at the address listed in Appendix A.

The Politics of Herbalism

Although herbalism has been practiced pretty much in the same manner for thousands of years, finding recognition through established health industry channels in this country could take another millennium or two, American herbalists believe.

Roy Upton says: "There is a monopolistic control of health care in this country. Things like midwifery, which is accepted worldwide, or herbalism, which is also accepted worldwide by other cultures, are not warmly embraced in this country. But that's changing.

"Presently, there are only two mechanisms by which someone can be licensed to practice medicine and utilize herbs in his or her practice. The first is to become licensed as a naturopathic physician. Naturopathic physicians are fully trained through medical schools and are called N.D.'s, as opposed to M.D.'s. Naturopathic medicine is essentially the practice of health by utilizing the principles of nature, such as diet, exercise, and herbal medicine.

"The other way to become licensed to use herbs is as an acupuncturist. Acupuncture is a foundation of Chinese medicine, and herbalism plays a large role in that discipline. But it has to be through a program that teaches herbal medicine. Not all acupuncture programs do."

What an Herbalist Does

Herbalists are familiar with the medicinal properties of various herbs and know which herbs can help with particular physical or emotional problems. However, unless they are licensed in either of the two above-mentioned categories, they cannot hang out a shingle and practice medicine in this country, even if in that practice all they are doing is recommending herbal teas.

According to Roy Upton: "Under the FDA, the federal Food and Drug Administration, you cannot legally dispense a substance for medicinal use unless that substance has been approved by the FDA. If you give garlic to someone, for example, and tell him or her that it can help lower cholesterol levels, you can be arrested for dispensing illicit drugs. Garlic.

"But we are pushing the system to change."

If you walk into any nutrition and health store you'll see rows of bottles and vials holding all the different herbs in their various forms. In essence, they are selling non-FDA-approved substances, which are therefore considered illegal. How do manufacturers and retailers buck the system?

The answer is simple. The products are not packaged as medicines; they are called "foods." (You can read more about careers in natural food stores in Chapter Five.)

Trained herbalists know what to do with these "foods." They are aware of how the popular medications used in this country—aspirins and sedatives, for example—can be substituted safely with common plants.

"Aspirin was originally derived from a plant called meadowsweet," Roy explains. "The Latin name at that time was spirea, which is where the 'spir' in 'aspirin' came from. So, if someone has a headache, for example, we would use a natural source, a tea made with meadowsweet.

"With sedatives, there are more than a million prescriptions written for Valium every year, which involves a $65 doctor visit and a $30 prescription, not to mention all the harmful implications. Instead, we would start with using something as simple as chamomile tea, which is what Peter Rabbit's mother gave him. Chamomile is a flower that has essential oils. These oils have calming and sedative properties. There are a whole range of calming herbs that get progressively stronger—from chamomile to skullcap to valerian root."

Herbalists get their message across without resorting to breaking the law. They teach and write books and articles, they lecture and offer apprentice programs, or they work for herbal product manufacturers.

Jobs with Herbal Product Manufacturers

There are several job titles available within the herbal product manufacturing industry:

- Research and development of products, developing formulas and processing techniques.

- Quality control, ensuring that the plants being used are the right plants, that they are not contaminated, and that they have the potency you want them to have.

- Writing literature to describe the products.

- Teaching classes to increase consumer awareness about the different products.

Pharmacognosy

Pharmacognosy is the study of the medicinal actions of plants and other natural products. It doesn't cover, as herbalism does, the practice of herbal medicine or the picking of medicinal plants. The related discipline pharmacology is the study of the medicinal actions of substances in general.

It is the job of pharmacognosy professionals to pick the product apart and study its constituents. Roy Upton explains: "Native American herbalists, for example, might not know that a plant contains volatile oils, alkaloids, and polysaccharides. They don't care about that. They know how to use it, how it works, and that's what's important.

"A pharmacognosist would study those elements, though they wouldn't necessarily know how to use them. The end result of their study is to try to develop synthetic drugs from the natural substances.

"Like herbalism, pharmacognosy was sort of an endangered species. At one time, physicians were trained in botany because they needed to know where their medicines came from. But then there was the separation between pharmacy and medicine, and other subspecialties were created, such as pharmacology and pharmacognosy, which kept on studying medicinal plants. As the chemical revolution took place in the 1800s, there was a big push to develop medicines as patentable substances in order to create a pharmaceutical industry. The craft of the herbalist and the pharmacognosist was less valued. Doctors no longer studied botany, and the thrust was to synthesize medicinal plants so they could be standardized to a certain level of activity. The professions almost died. It's only been in the last twenty years that there's been a resurgence."

The University of Illinois has one of the most widely recognized training programs in the country in pharmacognosy.

Horticultural Therapy

Any health nut who loves plants can tell you that being close to the soil—working with plants or just sitting in a fragrant and colorful spot—has therapeutic value. Horticultural activity has been long known to relieve tension, improve our physical condition, and promote a sense of accomplishment, pride, and well-being.

The earliest physicians in ancient Egypt prescribed walks in the garden for their mentally ill patients. The early American physician Benjamin Rush, who signed the Declaration of Independence, encouraged his psychiatric patients to tend gardens. In 1879, Pennsylvania's Friends Asylum for the Insane (today renamed Friends Hospital) built the first known greenhouse for use with mentally ill patients. And after World War II, veterans hospitals—with the help of scores of garden club volunteers—also promoted similar activity for their patients.

Today, horticultural therapy is an emerging science based on this time-tested art. In 1955, Michigan State University awarded the first undergraduate degree in horticultural therapy, and in 1971, Kansas State University established the first graduate program in the field.

What is Horticultural Therapy?

Horticultural therapists use activities involving plants and other natural materials to rehabilitate and/or improve a person's social, educational, psychological, or physical adjustment.

Therapists work with people who are physically or developmentally disabled, the elderly, drug and alcohol abusers, prisoners, and those who are socially or economically disadvantaged.

Charles A. Lewis of the Morton Arboretum says: "Plants possess life-enhancing qualities that encourage people to respond to them. In a judgmental world, plants are nonthreatening and nondiscriminating. They are living entities that respond directly to the care that is given them, not to the intellectual or physical capacities of the gardener. In short, they provide a benevolent setting in which a person can take the first steps toward confidence."

Horticultural therapists, in addition to utilizing standard gardening routines, also introduce alternative methods that are sensitive to the special needs of patients. This involves building wide paths and gently graded entrances and constructing raised beds to make gardening accessible to wheelchairs. Tools are also adapted; short handles, for example, work best with wheelchair-bound individuals, long handles for those with weak backs.

Job Outlook

Because of the continued growth of horticultural therapy, the demand for trained therapists has continued to rise. Horticultural therapists find work in rehab hospitals, nursing homes, substance abuse treatment centers, prisons, and botanical gardens and through inner city programs.

Finding that Job

Kansas State University in Manhattan, Kansas, maintains a job bank, and the American Horticultural Therapy Association (AHTA) lists openings its members post.

Some positions find their way into the Help Wanted section of local newspapers, but most horticultural therapists learn about positions through word of mouth—or they create their own.

Often, rehab centers, hospitals, and other appropriate settings aren't aware of the benefits of a horticultural therapy program. Enterprising therapists with PR skills have learned how to convince administrators that their services are needed.

Many begin by volunteering their time, working with patients or clients at the hospitals or through a local botanical garden.

That's how Nancy Stevenson got her start over twenty years ago.

What It's Like to Be a Horticultural Therapist

Nancy Stevenson earned a bachelor's degree in political science, then later went on for a master's in human services and became registered by the American Horticultural Therapy Association.

"I got interested in horticultural therapy back in the early seventies when it was still just a fledgling profession," Nancy explains. "The national organization, AHTA, was founded in 1973. At first I was a volunteer at a boys' detention center, working with someone who had started an indoor gardening program there. My colleague, Libby Reavis, whom I've been working with since then, volunteered with me. We got more and more interested and realized there was a real need in Cleveland to develop some training for this field. We worked through the Garden Center of Greater Cleveland (now known as the Cleveland Botanical Garden) to get some workshops going. We stayed as volunteers until 1981, then Libby and I joined the staff, sharing a full-time job between us. We went to them and said that this has gotten too big for us to handle as volunteers. We're spending twenty hours a week apiece on this. If you want to expand this any more and really get into horticultural therapy in a big way, you need a paid position. We helped them design the job and set the salary.

"Over the years we've had quite a varied program through the garden center. We contract with different agencies for outreach programs. Typical programs have been at children's hospitals or nursing homes. We'd go every other week and design a year-long curriculum that includes indoor and outdoor gardening. We have activities that involve propagation from seeds and cuttings, or repotting activities. We work with plants as well as dried materials for crafts, pressed flowers and flower arranging and that sort of thing.

"A good 60 percent of our time is spent out in the community. We recently developed a three-year program of intergenerational gardening in a neighborhood center in the inner city. The program brings seniors and elementary school children together.

"We also do a lot of public speaking to garden clubs and civic organizations to help educate people about horticultural therapy and its benefits."

Nancy also has been involved with training future horticultural therapists through the Cleveland Botanical Garden, which offers a six-month internship program. The address is listed in Appendix B.

The Rewards of the Profession

"It certainly isn't money," Nancy Stevenson says. "We're not very well paid. I think the reward for me is being able to combine horticulture and gardening, which have always been very strong interests of mine, with working directly with people—helping people learn about the therapeutic benefits of gardening and how working with plants can help them, no matter what their disability or limitation is.

"I think the relationship between therapist and client is very important. You set up a nonthreatening situation where positive change can occur for someone. You have to build trust."

Friends of Horticultural Therapy

In addition to Nancy's active role in the AHTA—she was president from 1989 to 1992 and only recently retired from the board—she is also chairperson of the Friends of Horticultural Therapy, which is an adjunct to the professional organization. "We're involved with public information and fund-raising," Nancy explains, "and one of our main purposes is to spread the good word about gardening as therapy—for everyone."

Members of the Friends of Horticultural Therapy help support the goals of the professional association, but they also receive a quarterly newsletter and discounts on garden supplies, seeds, and magazines, as well as special rates on conferences, tours, and seminars. You can contact the AHTA at the address listed in Appendix A.

The Training You'll Need

Because horticultural therapy is such a young discipline, finding training is not an easy process. Currently, Kansas State University's Department of Horticulture, Forestry and Recreation Resources is the only bachelor's and master's degree program offered in horticultural therapy in the United States. Three universities—Herbert H. Lehman College, Texas A & M University, and University of Rhode Island (program addresses can be found in Appendix B)—offer bachelor's degrees in horticulture with options in horticultural therapy. Edmonds Community College in Lynnwood, Washington, awards a two-year associate's degree in horticultural therapy, and various other institutionss such as Massachusetts Bay Community College and Temple University offer horticultural therapy electives.

An aspiring horticultural therapist can take several routes to become qualified. Dr. Richard Mattson, a professor at Kansas State University's program, recommends a four-year course of study that covers several disciplines.

"Originally, our program was narrowly defined in that we were training students to work primarily in psychiatric hospitals with mentally ill patients. We have a much broader definition today of horticultural therapy. It's more universal. We feel that the human benefits of gardening that deal with mental improvement such as self-esteem and stress reduction and social issues improving the quality of life that horticultural therapy is any kind of interaction of people and plants for mutual benefit. So, we work in community gardens or community farmer's markets. Students work in botanical gardens or arboreta, in the public school systems, or within zoo horticulture. They work in vocational training centers, in horticultural industry, or take international placements with the Peace Corps.

"Our concept at Kansas State is that the individual must be trained in a multidisciplinary approach," Dr. Mattson explains. "That means you have to cross over some of the traditional barriers that exist between discipline areas. For example, horticulture is one of the disciplines. Horticulture involves the art and science of growing and culturing plant material in intensive or adapted environments. But then, to work effectively with people, the student must be well-trained in psychology, sociology, and education. We think all of those are important. There are also supporting areas such as human ecology, which used to be called home economics. But it's a very important field because it deals with the growth and development of family and relationships. Architecture is also important for creating accessible landscapes. Students can also pursue a number of other areas such as speech pathology, communications, computer science, robotics, and human anatomy and muscle movement."

Also through the auspices of Kansas State's program, students spend a six-month internship gaining practical on-the-job training. Students are supervised by registered horticultural therapists in established programs and are placed coast to coast, from Friends Hospital in Philadelphia to the Chicago Botanical Gardens.

A four-year degree, although desirable, is not necessary to find work as a horticultural therapist. "There are different levels of entry into the field," says Dr. Mattson. "In this country there are a lot of volunteers who belong to garden clubs and master gardener groups taught by the Cooperative Extension Service. There are some programs that train at the Associate Arts level, for people who don't have the extra time to devote to their training. But I do think that the bachelor's or master's is important. At some time in the future the entry for many areas of employment in horticultural therapy will be at the graduate level. Horticultural therapy is not just making flower arrangements or planting gardens. We feel that multidiscipline training will help individuals apply what's best known in all the related fields. A good example is the importance of business and marketing skills. Many horticultural therapy programs today are cost-effective; that is, they are self-sufficient. But in order to utilize the valuable products being produced—whether sacks of potatoes from a vegetable garden or flowers or a landscaping service being provided—an individual needs some kind of skills in how to market the product."

The Registration Process

Although not every employer of horticultural therapists requires registration, being a registered therapist greatly increases your chances of landing a good job. Registration provides the individual with recognition as an accomplished therapist who has received the recognized training and helps to keep the profession's standards high.

There are three levels of registration: The H.T.T. designation is for the technician who has generally gone through a two-year program; the H.T.R. designation is for someone with a bachelor's degree; and the H.T.M. is for the person with a graduate degree and several years of experience.

However, becoming a registered horticultural therapist does not require a degree in horticultural therapy. A degree in a related field or a combination of work experience and education can all lead to professional registration.

Decisions about registration are peer-reviewed by a committee from the American Horticultural Therapy Association. The committee members follow a point system, awarding points for the number of years of experience, for publications, for attending seminars, for the number of degrees earned, and for other related activities.

Do You Have What It Takes?

In addition to training and experience, horticultural therapists need to have a certain personality makeup.

Nancy Stevenson describes the ideal therapist personality: "It's usually someone who's fairly outgoing and comfortable with people and able to express him or herself well. You should have a natural bent for teaching and be able to communicate with people to instruct them on basic gardening techniques. It's kind of an elusive quality, but you should have whatever that something is that makes people feel comfortable with you, to be able to talk freely with you. It's similar to the qualities most kinds of therapists should possess.

"I think you also have to be able to stay fairly detached and not get too emotionally involved with the people you're trying to help; otherwise, it can be hard on you."

Salaries for Horticultural Therapists

The American Horticultural Therapy Association conducts an annual survey to determine salary levels for nonregistered therapists, H.T.T.'s, H.T.R.'s, and H.T.M.'s. The results of a 1993 poll show that the average salary of therapists with one year or less employment experience is $24,920 per year. Averages go up with the number of years of working experience. Therapists can expect to make an average of $26,756 with one to five years of experience, $27,263 with five to ten years of experience, and $33,070 with ten or more years' experience.

Salaries increase by $1,500 to approximately $2,500 per year of additional work experience for those who have obtained professional registration.

CHAPTER FOUR

Let's Get Physical

P hysical fitness is important to most health nuts. In
addition to carefully monitoring what food they eat,
fitness-minded health nuts make time for regular exercise. They walk, jog, take aerobics classes, ride bicycles, participate in sports, or work out at health clubs or gyms.

For health nuts with athletic ability, what could be more
ideal than to incorporate their love of physical fitness into a
rewarding career? As trainers, instructors, coaches, and recreation workers, these skilled athletic types organize and lead
programs and watch over recreational facilities and equipment.
They help people to pursue their interests in sports or body
building for the purpose of entertainment, physical fitness, and
self-improvement. As physical, occupational, or recreational
therapists, they help people with physical limitations to reach
their full potential.

Working Conditions for Recreation Professionals

Recreation workers must work while others engage in leisure
time activities. Depending upon the setting, the majority of
workers put in a forty-hour week, but many of those hours can
be spent in the evenings or on weekends. Jobs can also be seasonal, such as at summer camps or with certain sports.

Most of the working hours are spent out of doors, although
recreational supervisors have more desk work and less physical
activity.

Training and Qualifications

The training and qualifications required for the different fields could range from a high school diploma (or less for some summer camp jobs) to a bachelor's or master's degree for supervisory or management positions.

A background in a specialty such as athletics or karate is usually a must. Some jobs also require special certificates such as lifesaving certification for water-related activities or teacher's certification for physical education instructors working in the school systems.

Associate's and bachelor's degree programs are offered throughout the country in parks and recreation, leisure studies, fitness management, and related disciplines.

The ideal recreation worker should be outgoing, creative, good at motivating people, and sensitive to the needs of others. Good health and physical fitness, needless to say, are also required.

Job Settings for Recreation Workers and Physical Fitness Buffs

Athletic health nuts can find full- and part-time work in a variety of settings. And while with some jobs relocation is a must to further a career, physical fitness experts need only take a walk through the neighborhood or scan the Yellow Pages to find employment close to home.

The following is a list of possible job settings. You can read more about each setting throughout this chapter.

- Cruise Ships

- Health Clubs, Spas, and Gyms

- Adult Education Programs

- Parks and Recreation Departments

- National Park Service (You can read about careers in the National Park Service in Chapter Seven.)

- Summer Camps

- YMCA, Boy Scouts, Red Cross

- Schools, Colleges, and Universities

- Hospitals

- Nursing Homes

- Rehab Centers

- Clinics

Working on a Cruise Ship

Probably everyone, at one time or another, has seen reruns of "The Love Boat" on television and watched Julie, Doc, Issac, Gopher, and Captain Steubing go about their daily activities, interacting with passengers while ensuring that they have the best vacations of their lives.

Although the reality might not exactly mirror life on the popular series, being part of a cruise ship staff can be fun and exciting, with the opportunity to travel to exotic ports, meet all different kinds of people, and lead a carefree lifestyle.

Job titles and responsibilities vary from ship to ship. For example, the term "cruise staff" is often synonymous with assistant cruise director or social or activities director.

Although filled with its share of excitement and glamour, working on a ship involves a lot of hard work. Cruise staff put in long hours—anywhere from eight to fifteen hours a day, seven days a week—and must maintain a high level of energy and always be cordial and friendly to passengers.

Cruise staff members are generally involved with organizing activities and social events, including common shipboard games such as shuffleboard and ring toss, Bingo, aerobics classes, basketball, golf putting (and driving—off the stern of the ship), and pool games. They also participate in cocktail parties and masquerade balls and take every opportunity to make sure passengers feel comfortable and are enjoying themselves.

Many of the cruise staff also double as entertainers and need to have some talent for performing, whether as singers, musicians, or deejays.

When in port, most of the crew are allowed to go ashore and have time off to explore, although some cruise staff function as chaperones, helping passengers find their way around foreign locales.

Activities aboard ship usually follow a rigid schedule, with little time in between for the crew to rest and take a break. With a constant eye on their watches, cruise staff run from one activity to another, announcing games over the loudspeaker, setting up the deck for exercise classes, supervising ring toss tournaments or other special events, and encouraging everyone to participate.

An outgoing, energetic individual would be in his or her element in such a job; someone who lacks those traits might find the work very difficult.

The Rewards

While salaries are not overly generous, the additional benefits are. Cruise staff are provided with free housing while on board ship and all they can eat. It's not necessary for a full-time employee of a cruise line to maintain quarters ashore, and, therefore, most of the salary can be saved.

Cruise ships also sail to exotic ports, giving staff members the chance to travel and meet people from all over the world.

Training for Cruise Staff Positions

A college education is not necessary, but some cruise lines prefer to see an applicant with a degree in psychology, hotel management, physical education, or communications. It's also a good idea to know another language, especially Spanish or German.

Even more important are the following personal qualities a good cruise staff should possess:

- Patience

- Diplomacy

- Tolerance for a wide variety of people

- A never-ending supply of energy

- An outgoing and genuinely friendly nature

- Enthusiasm

- Artistic talent

- Athletic ability

Most successful applicants land their jobs by applying directly to the various cruise lines, which are located mainly in Miami, Fort Lauderdale, Los Angeles, San Francisco, and New York. Look through the Yellow Pages in each city for cruise line addresses and phone numbers or consult *How To Get A Job with a Cruise Line*, mentioned in Appendix C.

Beverley Citron, Assistant Cruise Director

Beverley Citron began working on cruise ships at the age of twenty-one as a hairdresser. Realizing she would enjoy being part of the social staff more, she took time off to gain the necessary skills. Her hard work paid off and she landed her first job as a youth counselor. She also worked as a sports director, then was promoted to assistant cruise director.

Beverley talks about her job and how she got started: "I've wanted to work on a ship since I was five years old. I was influenced by two of my uncles who were in the English Royal Navy. Every time they came ashore they'd show me home movies they'd taken of the blue waters of Australia or Hong Kong. All through my school years it was my goal.

"I worked as a social director for a holiday resort and my local sailing club in England looking after children, planning and implementing their activities. I studied singing and the guitar, then put together an act with musical arrangements and costumes. I was determined to get a job as a social staff member.

"The cruise staff are in charge of all the games, activities, and shore excursions for the passengers. In a way, it's similar to being a camp counselor, but for adults. Youth counselors, of course, work with children.

"We make sure the passengers are having fun, and we try to come up with activities and events to capture their interest. We might organize a grandmother's tea or give an origami (paper folding) demonstration, or stage a treasure hunt. When in port, we might chaperone a group of passengers on a tour.

"Even between scheduled activities, we constantly interact and socialize with the passengers.

"Working on a cruise ship is my dream job. Every morning I always looked forward to getting up and starting the day. I'm not an office person; it's very difficult for me to stay at a desk all day. I've got a lot of energy and it's great for me being able to move about the ship making lots of friends, being busy.

"The people you work with become like a family. Sometimes you have to share a cabin and you become very close. Some people worry that working on a cruise ship would be a little like solitary confinement in a prison, that they wouldn't be allowed off of the ship for weeks at a time. But that's hardly the case. When you arrive in port, you always have an opportunity to go ashore. You can go to the beach, shopping, to nightclubs, discos. There are no days off while you're at sea, but you make up for that when you're in port.

"But the downside is you end up watching the clock all day. You have to be on the sports deck by 9 A.M., down in the lounge by 9:30, getting ready in your cabin to be back up on the deck by 10, and so on. You're on a rigid time schedule.

"You have to be constantly energetic and cheerful, even when you don't feel like it. You could work up to fifteen hours a day, but what else are you going to do? The alternative is sitting in your cabin."

Health Clubs, Spas, and Gyms

Health clubs, spas, and gyms offer employment to a large number of qualified health nuts. Job titles include the following:

- Personal Trainer

- Fitness Instructor

- Aerobics Instructor

- Racquetball/Squash Instructor

- Masseur/Masseuse

- Nutritionist (see Chapter Five)

To meet safety standards and insurance and state and local regulations, most health club-type settings require that their instructors and trainers have appropriate qualifications or licenses.

Many of the professionals in this setting hold a great deal of responsibility for their clients' welfare and must be fully trained in what they do.

Frank Cassisa, Certified Personal Trainer

Frank Cassisa is a certified personal trainer at Bally's Scandinavian Health and Tennis Corporation in Boca Raton, Florida.

Frank talks about his work: "Fitness instruction is just like computers; it's always changing, there's always something new coming out. To be the best trainer you have to stay on top of everything.

"You also need a great attitude and you have to practice what you preach. To clients you're a friend, father figure, role model. They'll follow someone who has the results they're looking for.

"Caring is also important. You need a firm hand but diplomatic skills. You're an instructor, not a dictator.

"One of the best settings is working in a health club. You don't have to generate business because the business is already there in the club. You can also have a private practice, at your own place or going to people's home. But once you're outside of a club setting you're talking totally different insurance coverage. If you work out of your own home or in a client's home you need to cover yourself. You're more open for a lawsuit, God forbid something happened to the client. At a club you come under the club's insurance.

"I work for Bally's and I'm covered by their insurance, but even then it doesn't mean someone couldn't come after me personally. But it would have to be plain stupidity to do something that could cause a client to get hurt. Safety is the key.

"We have to check the equipment before the client actually uses that equipment. You have to be fully aware of the human body and how it should move and shouldn't move. If there are any complications or special populations you're working with— diabetics, for example, or rehab cardiac patients, people with arthritis, or pregnant women—there are different ways to train them.

"When you're a certified personal trainer you're not only learning about nutrition and kinesiology, which is the study of the movement of the body and how the muscles react to certain exercises, you also learn first aid. All certified personal trainers must be certified in CPR.

"With the general population, people who want to improve their fitness, you first have to take a health history, get their doctor's name and number and ask the right questions—age, smoking, any history of health risk factors. If we feel certain people are not ready for a training program we'll tell them 'no' and have them contact their doctor for a physical.

"The perfect scenario for someone not ready is the forty-five-year-old male who smokes, is overweight, and somebody in his family had diabetes. This person could be a walking time bomb. It would be up to the doctor to do a stress test and see if he's ready. We don't do any diagnosing; we can only suspect. We're not doctors or dietitians; we have to refer them to professionals if we feel we can't answer their questions or if their condition needs medical attention.

"If the client is a go-ahead, we assess him and try to get in all the elements of physical fitness such as flexibility, muscular strength and endurance, cardiovascular endurance, and body composition. Normally a training session is an hour. Clients come once or twice a week to meet with the trainer. And they should come on their own the other days.

"For me it's my hobby and I'm getting paid for it. I love to work out and I love to teach people. I work five days a week. When I take my two-hour lunch break I'm working out. You have to be driven and absorb the whole lifestyle."

Salaries for Personal Trainers

Personal trainers in a health club can work on commission or an hourly rate, earning anywhere from $45 to $150 an hour, depending upon the budget of the clientele.

Says Frank: "You can work your own hours. You can train four people in a day and you're done. Over a week you're doing pretty well. But if you're self-employed, you have your taxes and insurance expenses, too."

Training for Trainers

There are a few routes trainers can take to learn their craft and become certified. Some universities offer exercise science or exercise physiology programs. You can also do a home study course through the American Council on Exercise (ACE), then sit for the exam given twice a year. The American College of Sports Medicine (ACSM) is also a certifying body. Both tests have written and practical components.

The practical test consists of sub-max testing, in which you are evaluated while you monitor a client's heart rate and blood pressure. You will also put your client through a workout, and your spotting techniques and how you interact will also be judged.

Once you have become a personal trainer you'll need continuing education credits to keep up your certification. A training program can take two weeks, eight weeks, or four years, if you pursue a bachelor's degree.

For more information on training and certification you can contact ACE and ACSM, which are both listed in Appendix A.

Adult Education Programs

Most communities offer a regular series of adult education or continuing education classes, usually held in the evenings at local schools or at adult education facilities, where classes can be offered during the day as well.

Depending upon their specialty, some instructors will need to apply for certification through the state school board. In that case, most program directors will walk their job applicants through the process. Other specialties require only that you demonstrate some expertise and an ability to instruct.

A look through the adult education class listings in your community will give you an idea where you might be able to fit in. Some courses regularly offered that would appeal to health nuts include:

- Dance Instruction (anything from line dancing to ballet or ballroom dancing)
- Gymnastics
- Scuba Diving
- Boating Safety
- Sailing
- Aerobics
- Karate
- Yoga

Pay is usually hourly and based on your education and experience. Although for the most part this field offers only part-time employment, teaching an adult ed class is a way for health nuts to share their knowledge, stay fit, and earn extra income at the same time.

Parks and Recreation Departments

Most cities have parks and recreation departments through which various activities are offered to the public at little or no cost. Many of the same classes offered through adult education are offered here as well, providing instructors and coaches with additional opportunities for employment.

In addition to a wide variety of sports—from tennis and football to volleyball and soccer—many Little League teams originate through parks and recreation departments.

Summer Camps

Camp counselors lead children and teenage campers in out-door-oriented forms of recreation, such as swimming, hiking, and horseback riding. Counselors also provide campers with specialized instruction in activities such as archery, boating, gymnastics, and tennis. At overnight camps, counselors are also responsible for supervising daily living tasks and general social-ization.

The pay is usually low but free room and board are always provided. Camp counseling is an excellent opportunity for college students to gain skills and earn extra money during summer vacations.

YMCA, Boy Scouts, and Red Cross

These organizations, and other similar enterprises, also provide recreation and sports activities for children and adults. Recre-ation workers and instructors can find work based at their in-town facilities or at day camps and resident camps located in country settings.

Schools, Colleges, and Universities

Most educational institutions require students to participate in some form of physical education, whether individual activities such as swimming or gymnastics or team sports such as basket-ball or football. Opportunities exist here for physical education teachers and athletic coaches.

Within primary and secondary education, physical education teachers are required to have at least a bachelor's degree and a teaching certificate issued by the state. Athletic coaches usu-ally are required to teach another subject—English, math, or science, for example—in addition to their coaching duties.

At the college level, physical education teachers might be required to have a master's degree. Coaches are generally sought out who have a good track record of successful wins.

Other careers for sports-minded people include sports medicine and sports psychology, highlighted in Chapter Two.

The "Therapies"

Although many health nuts prefer to work with a well population, there are also many who derive great satisfaction from helping those with physical or emotional limitations. Careers in this category include physical, occupational, and recreational therapy.

Physical Therapy

The purpose of physical therapy is to correct muscular-skeletal dysfunction and problems with movement. The physical therapist works independently, evaluating patients and designing and implementing treatment plans.

Physical therapists work with the following patients or problems:

- Premature infants

- Pediatric patients

- Obstetric patients

- People with sports or traumatic injuries

- People with birth or genetic defects

- People with back or neck injuries

- Stroke victims

- Burn and wound victims

- Amputees

- Dancers and performing artists
- Athletes
- People with muscular sclerosis, Parkinson disease, or neurological injuries
- Post-op patients
- Geriatric patients

Settings for Physical Therapists

While those not in the know might think of physical therapists as working only in hospital settings, in actuality, there is a wide range of settings open to physical therapy professionals. In addition to seeing patients in acute-care hospitals, both inpatient and outpatient, physical therapists see patients in their homes, providing home health care; in schools, working with students on the playing fields; in nursing homes; in rehab hospitals; in private practices; and in industry, doing job-site analyses that help prevent injuries. As an example, IBM or another large corporation could hire a physical therapist to evaluate risks the employees encounter, and then by taking the recommendations made by the physical therapist, can redesign the workplace and lower the number of worker compensation claims.

Physical therapists can also travel, working for what is called a traveling company. This kind of company will make sure you are licensed in whatever state you might go to, and then you will be sent around the country on temporary assignments, wherever there is a need.

Laurie DeJong, Physical Therapist

Laurie DeJong is assistant director of physical therapy at Boca Raton Community Hospital in South Florida.

She talks about the role of the physical therapist: "Physical therapists generally specialize, working in a particular setting or with certain kinds of patients.

"We evaluate patients, looking for pain, their flexibility or range of motion, their strength, and what kind of functional activities they do or need to do. For example, if the patient is a dancer, she needs to dance; if it's a child, she needs to play; if it's an adult, she needs to work, and so on. We do a complete evaluation, sitting down and talking to the patient about what the patient is looking for, about what we're looking for, and then, depending upon the person and her needs, we would design an appropriate treatment plan.

"Treatment plans generally include manual therapy, doing stretching or strengthening exercises, or specific joint mobilization exercises. We also use modalities such as hot packs, cold packs, ultrasound, or electric stimulation to help reduce pain.

"We do a lot of teaching, too, explaining the exercises to the patients so they can carry on the activities at home without us. We do a lot of education in terms of posture and how patients can prevent their injuries from recurring. If our patients are children, we also work with the parents or teachers, showing them how to do the exercises or how best to help the child function in the school arena. On the sports field we may be educating the coaches as to what kind of exercises a specific child needs.

"We also run classes, such as back schools and body awareness or risk management programs, within the hospital and within industry.

"Part of the job is doing documentation—that's the part most of us don't like, but it's necessary.

"As assistant director I supervise all physical therapy in the hospital, responsible for twenty P.T.'s and an additional fifteen aides. I do the hiring and work with the P.T.'s to develop their skills. I'm also responsible for developing and following the budget—what our expenses are, how much money we make— and ordering equipment.

"In addition, I personally see about fifteen patients a week.

"It's a great profession to have. You can specialize in so many different areas. We all come out with a basic background and then you can tailor your expertise to the area you prefer.

"In my job I like the fact that I can do a lot of different things. I can treat the kids, I can spend time hiring new staff members, I can go around the country to conferences meeting new people and seeing what the national trends are. I like the changing environment and the challenges of doing the budget and figuring out the finances. And I like being able to keep up with the changes in health care, keeping myself and my staff on the cutting edge of what's happening out there.

"The stresses are the same as for everyone else. There's not enough time to do the job you have to do. When supervising thirty-five people, you have thirty-five different personalities to deal with.

"It's also a challenge with the changes that are happening in health care. Some of the changes aren't fun and we don't like what's happening. There are now insurance companies telling us how we should treat our patients, as opposed to our dictating the kind of care our patients need. You'll find patients saying they know they need more treatment, but they won't be coming back to you because they can't afford it."

Laurie DeJong's Background

Laurie graduated in 1984 with a bachelor's degree in physical therapy from Quinnipiac College in Hamden, Connecticut. She spent four years working in a rehab hospital, and while there she started doing pediatrics and spent two years working with children as well as adults on an outpatient basis.

For one year she had her own private practice doing home health and consultation in schools. After moving to Florida she started as a staff physical therapist, then moved into administration.

"I always liked medical things," Laurie explains. "I started playing hospital when I was about two. My parents told me I couldn't be a nurse, but I could become a doctor if I wanted to. But when I was seventeen I realized how long it would take me to become a doctor.

"I honestly like the P.T. profession because we have a lot of hands-on time with our patients. We develop a treatment plan and then we see the patients generally two or three times a week for at least a month. I like working with the kids because I can see them for years. A child with developmental delays, such as cerebral palsy, for example, I'll see forever. We get to develop a rapport, spending time one-on-one with our patients. Doctors don't have the time to do that."

Training for Physical Therapists

Physical therapists must have at least a bachelor's degree. Some go on for a master's degree, and others earn a doctorate. Most schools require anywhere from twenty to one hundred hours of observation time before future P.T.'s can even apply to be admitted to a program. This observation time can be clocked while volunteering or working as a physical therapy aide. (This on-the-job training position is explained later in this chapter.) Physical therapy programs can be found through the American Physical Therapy Association, listed in Appendix A.

Course work covers mostly math and sciences as well as specific training on the techniques used in physical therapy, including exercise science and exercise physiology. Although the training is similar to that undertaken by personal trainers (see the interview with Frank Cassisa earlier in this chapter), physical therapy training is more medically based. Physical therapy students study more pathology, doing cadaver dissections, for example. The study of anatomy and physiology is more extensive, as is muscle pathology. But the differences are explained easily by the different people each works with. Personal trainers deal with a healthy population for the most part; physical therapists work with patients who have disabilities or a variety of other problems.

Physical Therapist Assistant

While the physical therapist is responsible for the design of treatment plans, the physical therapist assistant is trained to carry out those plans. Limitations for physical therapist assistants are that they cannot update or change treatment plans.

Training for a physical therapist assistant career involves a two-year program ending with an associate's degree.

Physical Therapy Aide

Physical therapy aides are usually trained on the job. They can't do direct patient care, but they help both the physical therapist and the physical therapist assistant. Aides might help a patient count the number of exercises he or she is doing, move equipment, bring patients to the treatment areas, or help a person walk or transfer from the bed to a chair.

Salaries in the Physical Therapy Profession

A brand new graduate physical therapist can make an excellent starting salary—between $35,000 to $40,000 a year, depending upon the region of the country in which you choose to practice. Salaries increase with the number of years' experience.

Physical therapists working in home health can make $40 to $50 an hour, and physical therapists in private practice can make between $85,000 and $100,000 a year. But these self-employed physical therapists have more expenses to cover, too, such as liability insurance. In private practice, a physical therapist has to wear many hats, one of which is that of bill collector. And it can be difficult sometimes to collect payments.

Traveling physical therapists usually make a good hourly salary and have all their expenses covered, including flights, rental cars, hotel rooms, and meals.

Physical therapy assistants with a two-year degree can start earning between $20,000 and $30,000 a year. The nonprofessional position of physical therapy aide earns about $5 an hour.

Job Outlook for Physical Therapists

The job outlook for physical therapists is excellent. There has been a shortage of physical therapists for quite awhile now. There are two main reasons for this. The capabilities and problems that the physical therapist is qualified to handle have expanded, creating more of a demand.

Secondly, because academia doesn't pay well, there is a shortage of qualified people willing to teach in physical therapy training programs. When the teacher makes less money than the student, there is little motivation to follow that career path. Physical therapists with doctorates are required to teach master's and doctoral-level students. The number of qualified teachers is very low. Most physical therapists prefer to work in the field than in a classroom. With fewer teachers, fewer physical therapists can be trained, thus contributing to the shortage and increasing the demand.

Occupational Therapy

The American Occupational Therapy Association defines occupational therapy as: "a health and rehabilitation profession. Its practitioners provide services to individuals of all ages who have physical, developmental, emotional, and social deficits, and because of these conditions, need specialized assistance in learning skills to enable them to lead independent, productive, and satisfying lives."

Helen Cox, Occupational Therapist

In the words of Helen Cox, an occupational therapy supervisor in the Rehab Services Department at Boca Raton Community Hospital in South Florida, "occupational therapy is a health profession that helps people to do things for themselves within the limits of their disability or disease."

How do occupational therapists do that? Helen explains: "First of all, we need to evaluate the patients to see what their skills are or where they have some deficits. Then we have to make a decision as to whether we can improve those deficits. For instance, if someone has had a stroke, and he or she has a weak arm on the side of the stroke, do we feel we can, through exercise and other activities, improve the function of the arm and get it back to what it was prior to the stroke?

"We have to see if patients have the motor ability, the muscle power, and the strength to perform any activities. Do they have the coordination? Sometimes they might have the motor power but they couldn't pick up a coin from the table. That means they would be limited in doing some things for themselves.

"Sometimes in the evaluation, we realize that with arthritic patients, for example, they have lost the ability to manipulate small buttons. Then we can look into some adaptive equipment such as button hooks, dressing sticks, or elastic shoelaces, which don't need as fine a motor ability to use.

"After the assessment we set realistic goals with the patient. 'Where do you want to be functioning in a month? Where do you want to be functioning in three or four months?' The goals may be as simple as putting on socks or a sweater, or as long range as being able to sew or play the piano.

"When we have the goals, we use various activities, from putting round pegs in round holes to maybe even practicing the piano or using a computer keyboard. It depends on what skills they're trying to develop.

"At the end of thirty days we evaluate the progress. We may have initially measured grip and pinch strength and then we'll measure them again to see if there's been improvement.

"If we haven't reached the goals, we look to see why. Maybe the patient had another stroke or something else interfered. If we do reach the goals, we make new short-term goals until the patient has reached his or her maximum potential.

"Being able to see people improve is the nicest part of the job. Sometimes patients surprise you with what they're able to accomplish."

Helen's Background

Helen originally planned to become a nurse. "I was away at college and was having problems with chemistry. My brother, who is a physical therapist, said to me, 'Why do you want to become a nurse, anyway, and work all those ridiculous hours on weekends, nights, and holidays?' My mom was a nurse and that's why I was pursuing it. My brother suggested I become an occupational therapist and I said, 'What's that?' He was working at a VA hospital, so I went there to visit the occupational therapy clinic. I saw that it was a lot of hands-on care, and then I knew that that's what I wanted to do."

Helen received her B.S. degree in occupational therapy from the University of Illinois in Chicago in 1970.

Training for Occupational Therapists

Occupational therapists must earn a four-year degree, studying all the sciences—zoology, biology, physiology, anatomy, kinesiology. You also take psychology, abnormal psychology, and child development classes. Specialties you can study are pediatrics, psychiatry, hands, and physical disabilities.

After your four years, you will do a six- to nine-month internship, rotating in different kinds of facilities and specialties. Once you pass your internship, there is a national exam you have to take to become a registered occupational therapist.

Some occupational therapists go on for master's degrees in occupational therapy or related fields such as administration or physical therapy.

The personality qualities and skills you'll need to make a good occupational therapist are as follows: You should be outgoing, with a lot of empathy and a good sense of humor. You'll need to be open and willing to talk with your patients. You also have to be a good listener. Patients look at their therapist as someone they can talk to—doctors rarely have enough time for that kind of relationship. You also need good people skills for dealing with coworkers and the family members of your patients.

Settings for Occupational Therapists

Occupational therapists work with all types of patients, from premature infants to geriatric patients, and with all kinds of diagnoses. This covers anything that would limit the patients' ability to care for themselves—arthritis, hand injuries, burns, neurological dysfunction. Such patients may be stroke victims or have multiple sclerosis, muscular dystrophy, cerebral palsy, brain tumors, or psychiatric problems.

Occupational therapists work in the following settings:

- Acute-care Hospitals

- Rehab Hospitals

- Psychiatric Hospitals or Wards

- Pediatric Hospitals or Wards

- Nursing Homes

- School Systems

- Private Practice

The Differences between Physical Therapists and Occupational Therapists

"We differ from physical therapists in a few ways," Helen Cox explains. "Although we have the same goals—to make the patient as independent as possible—physical therapists deal with only the patients' physical difficulties. Occupational therapists work with physical and psychosocial aspects. A lot of occupational therapists work in psychiatric facilities, helping patients to cope with their emotional problems. And some patients have a combination of problems. They might have had a stroke but are suffering from depression as well.

"And while we both deal with physical problems, we don't do it in the same way. An occupational therapist probably wouldn't help a person with ambulation skills, learning how to walk. However, both the physical and occupational therapist might focus on transfer skills, helping a person get from the bed to a chair, from the chair to a standing position."

Certified Occupational Therapy Assistants

Certified occupational therapy assistants study at a community college and earn a two-year associate's degree. Although they don't evaluate patients or make treatment plans, they function much as physical therapy assistants do, carrying out the plans made by the occupational therapists.

Some universities have started weekend programs for occupational therapy assistants who want to go ahead and get a four-year degree. While they are employed full-time, they study every other week-end, finishing the bachelor's degree in about two years.

Occupational Therapy Aides

Occupational therapy aides function similarly to their physical therapy counterparts, helping the occupational therapists and assistants with various duties.

Salaries for Occupational Therapists

Salaries for occupational therapists are similar to those for physical therapists and can start at an average of $35,000 a year. Starting salaries for certified occupational therapy assistants would average about $20,000 a year. Occupational therapy aides would earn from $5 to $5.50 an hour.

Recreational Therapy

Recreational therapists employ activities to treat or maintain the physical, mental, and emotional well-being of patients. Activities range from sports, games, and drama to arts and crafts and music. Recreational therapists also often organize field trips, taking patients bowling, to sporting events, or on picnics.

Recreational therapists work in acute-care hospitals, psychiatric hospitals, nursing homes, and rehab centers. Community-based recreational therapists work in parks and recreation departments, special education programs, and programs for the elderly or disabled.

In a clinical setting, recreational therapists work in conjunction with physicians, nurses, psychologists, social workers, and physical and occupational therapists.

Recreational therapists assess patients based on information in medical charts and from talking with other staff and family members as well as with the patients themselves. They then develop and carry out therapeutic activities consistent with the needs of the individual. For example, patients having difficulty with socialization skills may be included in games with other patients, or a right-handed person with a right-side paralysis after a stroke may be helped to use his or her left arm to swing a tennis racket or throw a softball.

Training for Recreational Therapists

A bachelor's degree in therapeutic recreation or in recreation with an option in therapeutic recreation is the usual requirement for hospital work and related clinical positions. Associate's degrees in recreational therapy; training in art, music therapy, or drama; or related work experience may be enough to qualify for activity director positions in nursing homes.

Courses students study include clinical practice and helping skills, program design, management, anatomy, physiology, abnormal psychology, medical and psychiatric terminology, characteristics of illness and disabilities, the concepts of mainstreaming and normalization, professional ethics, assessment and referral procedures, and the use of equipment.

In addition to the academics, recreational therapy students must participate in a 360-hour internship.

After earning the bachelor's degree, new grads take the exam put out by the National Council for Therapeutic Recreation Certification to become certified.

Salaries for Recreational Therapists

Recreational therapists generally start out in the high twenties or low thirties. Activity directors in nursing homes earn an average of $25,000 a year.

Other career paths for therapists include mental health counseling and psychotherapy (Chapter Two) and horticultural therapy (Chapter Three).

CHAPTER FIVE

The World of Food

T o a health nut, nothing is more important than eating good, healthful food. For health nuts hoping for a rewarding career related to their interests, there are many options in the world of food.

Health nuts wanting to work with food can find careers on organic farms, growing and marketing; with the Cooperative Extension Service as Extension Agents; in natural food stores supplying customers with information as well as products; in food co-ops; and in restaurants, preparing and serving healthful meals.

Other food-related careers include counseling people on diet and nutrition issues, discussed later in this chapter, and writing about food, highlighted in Chapter Six.

Growing Food

At the heart of our economic structure are American farmers, who operate one of the world's largest and most productive agricultural industries. They produce enough food to meet the needs of our country and to export huge quantities to countries around the world.

Farms can be huge conglomerates or small, privately or cooperatively owned enterprises. Farmers can also be tenant farmers, renting the land they use.

Duties in Agricultural Careers

Within the field of agriculture there are a number of different occupations. On the production side are the growers, owners, managers, and field hands. Once the food has been harvested, experienced handlers store it, then pack and ship it. Distributors handle sales and marketing, and retailers such as restaurants and supermarkets sell to the public.

The specific tasks for growers are determined by the type of farm. On traditional crop farms, operators are responsible for planning, tilling, planting, fertilizing, cultivating, spraying, and harvesting. Organic farmers, who do not use chemicals in their operations, must also seek out alternative ways to fight pests and disease and increase production.

On large farms, owners or managers spend time meeting with supervisors and traveling between the fields and their offices.

Training for Farmers

Modern farming requires complex scientific, business, and financial decisions. Today's farmer must acquire a strong educational background. No longer is it enough to grow up on a farm or participate as a youth in 4–H activities, though these are important contributors to an overall education.

For those who have no previous farming experience, a bachelor's degree in agriculture is essential. To qualify as a manager, several years' experience in different phases of farm operation would also be necessary.

Students should choose a college appropriate to their specific interests and locations. All states have land-grant colleges with agriculture departments. For crop growers, courses would cover agricultural economics, crop and fruit science, and soil science.

Farm operators and managers need to keep informed of continuing advances in farming methods. They should be willing to try new techniques and adapt to constantly changing technologies to produce or enhance their crops.

They should also be familiar with the different farm machinery and its safe use, as well as with chemicals and their applications.

Accounting and bookkeeping are also important skills. And these days, more and more farms are depending upon computers to keep track of accounts and crop production and distribution.

Farm managers need to have business skills, good communication skills, and marketing and sales experience.

Finger Lakes Organic Growers Cooperative

The Finger Lakes Organic Growers is a cooperative enterprise with approximately thirty active members. Most of the farms, which are spread across New York State, are fifteen acres or smaller. The growers purchased shares in the cooperative; in exchange, the cooperative markets their produce for them.

Their aim is to grow all their crops organically without the use of any chemical pesticides or fertilizers. They are committed to sustainable agriculture, meaning they farm in such a way that the environment benefits from it—the soil gets richer and the general ecology is preserved.

Carol Stull, Grower

Carol Stull is one of the founding members of the Finger Lakes Organic Growers Cooperative, which began operation in 1986. "It actually started under the black locust tree in my backyard," Carol explains. "There had been a group of growers, about six of us, who had been meeting and talking about how running around and trying to sell everything ourselves was a hassle. Several of our regular customers would buy one thing from someone, but if they ran out, they'd go to someone else. So our thinking was that if we could go together it would be more expeditious.

"We had been talking about it for a year and then one of the growers said, 'Let's do it and here's my $5 to start.' We used that money to mail out the minutes. Then we applied for a grant from New York State Agriculture and Markets. At the time they had money they'd gotten from the federal government for grants.

"We got $15,000 and we used it as start-up money for the cooperative. We set up a computer program and we rented a truck for deliveries. The market manager worked out of her living room then. That first year we didn't even have a warehouse—we used a farm that belonged to one of our growers, and we brought things there or to a couple of pickup points. We were pretty low-budget, but we were able to pay an artist to develop our logo and to get office supplies. And also, when you sell things, there's a delay between the time you sell and the time you get the money, so we used some of the grant to cover employees' salaries.

"Each member has his or her own farm. Right at the beginning one of the things we decided was that we couldn't compete with each other in the marketplace. We got advice from a Vista volunteer who worked with another cooperative and learned that we should, for example, set up a personnel committee so every grower wasn't telling the manager something different to do. We each gave up all our wholesale markets to the co-op. It used to cost us at least a quarter of our time to do the selling, and that really wasn't enough to do it right. So we've changed that now and the manager takes care of all of that."

Carol's Individual Farm

Carol and her husband bought their land in Ithaca, New York, in 1985. "Our business was only a year old when we started the cooperative. Before that we used to market our produce direct at farmer's markets. We were small, just learning to go from packets to pounds. You buy a packet of seeds for a small home garden, but when you're growing commercially you buy seeds by the pound. We have sixty-five acres and farm about ten acres of it. We grow all of the standard vegetables, except corn. We have a problem with deer.

"One of the reasons I like doing this is that I can grow any weird thing I want. That was one of our entries into the whole-sale restaurant market. I can grow edible flowers or unusual cherry tomatoes that other people don't grow. We also grow a lot of herbs—seven or eight different basils, for example.

"The number of employees I have fluctuates. In the summer I hire students. We have about eight who help with the plant-ing and picking. It's a lot easier if you have several thousand tomatoes plants and six or eight people to chat with as you're picking. Then it can be fun work. By yourself it's a lot harder.

"I do all the planning. We grow a lot of different crops, so we have to know where they're going to go. We do a three-year rotation, which means we don't plant crops from the same fam-ily in the same place in the field for three years.

"There's a lot of planning and a lot of adjusting to your plan-ning if things don't work out—whether it's the weather that doesn't cooperate or the equipment breaks down or someone doesn't show up or things grow faster or slower than you thought they would. You spend a lot of time figuring out what you're doing. We have 187 different food products and a wide line of perennials and herb plants, and that's a lot going on.

"We have three greenhouses, and in the winter I grow a lot of salad greens for the hotel school at Cornell University."

Carol also sells at the local farmer's market on Saturdays and has a roadside stand on her property. "When you have more cherry tomatoes than you absolutely know what to do with you look at every market available."

Carol's Background

Carol was trained as a clinical chemist with a biology back-ground. She worked eighteen years as a hospital chemist. Her bachelor's degree is from the University of Illinois and her master's is from Baylor in Texas.

Although she grew up in suburban Evanston, Illinois, there's been a farm in her family since her great grandfather's time.

Carol loves farming. "We have a very inspiring view. Our farm sits on top of a hill overlooking twenty miles of Cayuga Lake. If you're feeling a little down in the morning, the view will perk you up.

"But what I like most is the fascination of seeing a little seedling transfer into something big, watching the flowers open up, then seeing the fruits of your labor when you go out and start harvesting. The little plants you transplanted are now ready to be eaten or sold or whatever you're going to do with them. It's a thrill."

Sally Miller, Manager of Finger Lakes Organic Growers Cooperative

The Finger Lakes Organic Growers employ a full-time marketing manager, an assistant manager, and a warehouse manager who is responsible for quality control and putting the orders together to go out on the trucks. The work is seasonal, and the managers are on shorter schedules in the winter.

Sally Miller is the cooperative's marketing manager. "My main function is the marketing and advertising," Sally explains. "We try to expand the business. The board of directors meets once a month to do long-term strategic planning with our recommendations. If they decide they want to expand, say 20 percent with new customers, then it's the manager's job to decide how to do that."

Thousands of bushels go through the warehouse every year, and this year they're expecting to gross about $400,000 in sales.

"We supply to restaurants, supermarkets, retail food co-ops, and natural food stores, and to other wholesalers when we have a surplus of something. For example, zucchini tends to grow all at once and it's doing that right now. We have so much that I can lower the price and make it appealing to other wholesalers who might not have enough of a supply.

"Very few people do standing orders. The prices change every week and most restaurants change their side orders—that's what we supply—from week to week. And there's a lot of competition. All the customers get different price lists every week and then they decide who they're going to buy from. We fax price lists and follow up with a call. Some of our customers, such as Moosewood Restaurant, are nearby so we can figure out what they need and drop it off on our way home from work. Locally we know all the people we're selling to.

"For customers farther away we have an arrangement for shipping with the people we share warehouse space with. They're Regional Access, a natural food wholesaler, and we rent their truck. Often we ship to a lot of the same customers.

"In addition to the marketing, I do a certain amount of educating about new crops, how to store them and display them. We put out a newsletter and do all the bookkeeping—anything that goes into a business.

"One of the things our cooperative is famous for is very good hands-on quality control, so we spend a lot of time in the cooler examining the produce. Then, when a customer calls we can say that we have great red leaf lettuce, for example. The heads are small but they're holding together very well. We try to give a lot of information. Or we share information about what's moving well or not moving at different food co-ops. There are always trends. Asparagus is something people buy like crazy—they love it. So if you have asparagus you know they'll have no trouble selling it. But then something like chard, which was very popular when I first started working here—it's a gorgeous thing and has long leaves and you can chop it up and use it in stir fries—is becoming less and less popular and there's no real reason why.

"We end up talking about the weather a lot, too. People might mention casually that it's been real hot. And then we say, 'Yes, and that's why we don't have any lettuce. Not only are you suffering, but all of our lettuce has bolted—gone to seed—and it doesn't taste good anymore.

"We take the orders and keep track to make sure we're not running out of things. The warehouse manager comes in and gets the invoices and then goes into the cooler and stacks the boxes together on a truck pallet, ready to go out. Then our trucker loads up and drives off.

"Sometimes, things go wrong with the orders and we deal with that. Someone got something they weren't expecting or their bananas were too ripe and they want a discount. And there's always mediation between customers and growers. Your customers don't necessarily know how agriculture works; your growers don't understand marketing. So you help resolve any disputes."

Sally's Background

Sally spent eight years earning her doctorate in anthropology at Cornell University in Ithaca, New York. She finished in January, 1992, but by May she felt as if she'd had enough. "I realized I didn't want to spend my life teaching. I don't think I was really cut out for it. But the degree gave me a lot of experience that I use now—doing interviews, writing a project yourself, getting funding, and writing grants, which is a kind of marketing.

"I had done a lot of volunteer work at Greenstar, the local food co-op. I loved it and realized that that was what I wanted to do. Originally, I was looking for a farming job but there weren't any, then this job came along and I started in May of 1992.

"What I'm doing here seems more real for me. In some ways it was a political decision. I feel I'm doing more now because I'm working with a lot of people who are doing sustainable agriculture, trying to preserve the land and not putting pesticides into the air. Organic farming is a very difficult business;

they tend to be small family farms and they go out of business all the time. So if I can sell a lot of their produce and get good prices for them, then maybe that's one farm that doesn't go out of business this year.

"I love marketing, talking to the customers. Some of them I've known for a long time and they trust me to make sure their produce looks good. And I trust them to go on buying from me and not switch to other suppliers. You tend to develop good relationships that way.

"There's some stress to the job. Last week we had 150 cases of lettuce come in and that was about twenty times the amount we had the week before. I was worried about whether or not it would all sell, but it was exciting, too. And it did all sell.

"If it hadn't sold, I would've had to tell the growers and then compost it all. If you've had a stressful day it's a good way to get over it, carrying out the slimy lettuce to the compost heap."

Earnings for Farmers

Income for farmers can vary from year to year. Food prices fluc-tuate from week to week and are affected by the weather and other factors that influence the demand for certain products.

The size and type of the farm also affects income. Generally, large farms produce more income than smaller operations. The exceptions to that are the specialty farms that produce small amounts of high-value horticultural and fruit products.

According to the U.S. Department of Agriculture, average income after expenses for operators of vegetable and fruit farms was $100,000 in 1993. Individual income can vary widely. Sally Miller, the manager of the Finger Lakes Organic Growers, earns $8.25 an hour; her assistant manager started out at $6.50 an hour and will go up to $7 or $7.50 after she's been on board for a while.

Carol Stull's seasonal workers earn between minimum wage and about $5 an hour. The growers within the cooperative earn different amounts depending upon the size of their property or what kind of year they had. The earnings could range from just $1,000 to about $35,000 to $40,000 in gross sales. Carol's own farm grosses about $25,000 to $30,000 a year.

"People don't realize how much it costs to grow food," Carol says. "I'm still selling things at the same price I was ten years ago because that's what people expect to pay. But ten years ago the minimum wage was lower; now it's gone up and I pay worker's comp and social security, too.

"It's what I do for a living, but my husband also has a full-time job outside the farm. I wouldn't be able to do this at this level if it were just me. As you pay off your equipment and mortgage you have a little more left over for your own salary, but it's not easy."

Because the work for some farmers and managers is seasonal, and the income fluctuates so, many growers take second jobs during the off months.

Job Outlook

Employment of farm managers and operators is expected to decline through the year 2005. With an expanding world population there is an increasing demand for food, but because of the efficiency of the American agricultural sector, fewer farms are needed to meet that demand. The overwhelming majority of job openings will come about because of the need to replace farmers who retire or leave the occupation for economic or other reasons.

The trend toward fewer but larger farms is expected to continue to reduce the number of jobs. Small- and medium-size farms, many of which do not generate enough income to support their owners, are expected to decrease in number.

However, the increase in the size of farms, generally through mergers, and the higher level of technology being employed in farm work are expected to spur a need for highly trained and experienced farm managers.

The Cooperative Extension Service

In the early 1900s the United States was largely an agrarian society. The farmers felt they needed more information about agriculture in order to do a better job feeding the nation. At that time approximately 40 percent of the population was spread out in rural areas, and the rest resided in urban centers. Now the proportions have changed, with only about 3 or 4 percent living in agricultural areas and rural settings.

A number of issues were brought before Congress at the time to help the nation's agricultural interests. First, a bill was passed forming land-grant colleges so that every state would have a college that would be technical in nature with its main focus to conduct research in agriculture.

Second, Congress recognized the need for physical locations in which to conduct related research. Because of the type of research needed, it couldn't be done in a laboratory, it had to be done out in the field. This brought about the establishment of research stations associated with each land-grant college. They were located at the universities, or nearby, wherever the crops were. In some states more than one research station was established.

Third, it was realized that with all this new research and knowledge being gained, there needed to be a way to disseminate the information. This is how the Cooperative Extension Service was born.

The title "Cooperative" was chosen because the program is funded with state, county, and federal monies. Every county has at least one, if not more, programs. An advisory board for each county points out areas that need to be addressed and services that need to be offered.

What the Cooperative Extension Service Does

The function of the Cooperative Extension Service has expanded beyond agricultural issues and now also covers home economics, the 4–H youth program, and a program which helps commercial fisheries.

The Cooperative Extension Service works with the community and tries to bring the research that's done at the universities to the public where it's needed. To do this, the Cooperative Extension Service employs professional agricultural specialists, horticulturists, and educators in the job title of Cooperative Extension Agent.

Loretta Hodyss, Cooperative Extension Service Agent

Loretta Hodyss has been a Cooperative Extension Agent in Palm Beach County, Florida, since 1979. "In a county like Palm Beach with a population of 900,000, maybe only 10,000 are associated with agriculture and the rest are urban," Loretta explains. "Therefore, the largest component of our work is urban horticulture. We answer people's questions about their lawns or how to grow a certain plant on the window sill or how to grow vegetables, trees, shrubs—whatever is needed. The service is free to the public, but we have to charge for some publications and classes to cover expenses."

Loretta works mainly with the county's commercial nursery industry. "I spend my time answering questions, helping them with their crop problems—mostly insect- and disease-related issues. In Palm Beach County it's a $200 million industry. We have 600 nurseries, which keeps me pretty busy.

"Some of my work I do over the telephone. We're open for questions from the public from nine to five, Monday through Friday. And although we can't do this for homeowners, very frequently I will go out to the nurseries to answer questions.

"We also have a lot of educational programs, all different sorts of classes, newsletters we send out, and published material we distribute. Whatever technical mechanism we can use to get the information out we do it."

Loretta likes having a challenging job with something different to do every day. "There's always something new and interesting to learn, and you're constantly encouraged to go back to school and learn. There is a wealth of information out there—and a wealth of people who are appreciative of your help.

"My role is that of educator more than anything else. Many of us do research, also. We've struggled with the title—we'd rather be called Extension Educators than Extension Agents, and in some states they have changed it."

Becoming a Cooperative Extension Agent

An Extension Agent is an employee of the land-grant college and the county. The position requires a master's degree in whatever field is appropriate—vegetable science, agriculture, entomology, pathology, or any related subjects. Loretta Hodyss has a master's in horticulture.

"There is a growing need for policy-making agents," Loretta explains, "people who will work with the community on environmental issues. These agents could be sociologists, for example. We're all called Extension Agents, but the job can cover a lot of different specialties.

"What we do is determined by the needs of the county. If they were growing wheat here I'd have to be a wheat specialist. If we had cows I'd need a vet/med background."

The number of agents varies with the county. In Loretta's office there are twelve agents. Five deal with home economics and the youth and fishermen programs; seven cover urban and agricultural horticulture.

"In some counties in Florida, there are affiliated positions that are called County Agents. The titles vary from state to state, but in Florida a County Agent is employed solely by the county. That position doesn't require a master's but it does require a bachelor's."

Every office also has a director to whom the Extension Agents report. To become a director, a master's degree is required as well as several years' experience working as an Extension Agent.

Willingness to work hard is also a requirement, Loretta explains: "You're on call twenty-four hours. Some of us carry beepers. I have a cellular phone that's always with me. That can be troublesome. If there's a hurricane or heavy rain or some disaster, we are expected to help and answer questions about what people should do in those situations. People rely on us heavily. That's what we want, but for some people it can be stressful.

"I find it gratifying, though. You need to be the kind of person who can deal with that."

Salaries for Extension Agents

Salaries follow state and county scales and vary from region to region. An affiliated agent with a bachelor's degree would expect to earn in the high teens. A new agent just out of graduate school could expect to earn $20,000 to $25,000 a year.

After a few years of experience, salaries increase with cost-of-living and merit raises.

Finding a Job with the Cooperative Extension Service

Although the Cooperative Extension Service has a national office in Washington, D.C., there is no national job bank. Positions are usually posted at the land-grant colleges, and the individual county offices are then notified.

Contacting the state university is the best place to start. You can find your local Extension Office in the telephone book under county or state government offices.

For those seeking a career with the Extension Service, it's a good idea to be prepared to relocate. You can decide upon an area of the country in which you would like to work, making sure you are familiar with the different horticultural requirements of that area. Then call the various land-grant colleges for job openings.

Natural Food Stores

Natural food stores are specialty shops that cater to health nuts, selling a wide range of healthful foods and related items such as vitamins and food supplements. Employees in natural food stores must be knowledgeable about the different foods and products and be able to answer a wide range of customer questions.

Cabbages Health Emporium

Cabbages Health Emporium opened its doors in 1991 as a market stocking health-oriented products. It offers a line of organic produce, organic foods, and nonorganic frozen foods and groceries. The Emporium avoids food with preservatives, refined sugars, or additives. It will not sell any food that has been irradiated to prolong its shelf life.

Cabbages Health Emporium customers are people with special diet or health needs, and those who just live a natural, healthy lifestyle, including vegans and vegetarians. The store has a cafe and a vegan deli and also caters to sports enthusiasts and body builders by stocking several lines of sports drinks and powders and different types of vitamins and formulas. In addition, the store carries a line of environmentally safe cleaning products that are biodegradable with no harsh chemicals.

Theresa Bulmer, Manager of Cabbages Health Emporium

Theresa joined the staff of Cabbages in 1994 and is now the store manager. Theresa talks about her work: "The duties of a manager vary from store to store. I do a little of everything. I do ordering, take out garbage, clean bathrooms, ring up sales, work on store operating policies, and talk to brokers, sales reps, and distributors six days a week from 7:30 in the morning to 6:00 at night. I also supervise ten employees.

"And I talk to customers and try to keep them happy. The customers are wonderful, really. They can learn from us and we can learn from them. Someone will come in with a product I've never seen before. I'll ask what they take it for and they'll rattle off everything the product can do and I get really excited because I'm learning something new.

"Some of our customers are real knowledgeable—sometimes even more knowledgeable than we are—and then we have those who are clueless. They tell us it's their first time in a health food store and they don't know what they should be buying. We're all customer service-oriented here, and if anyone is unable to help, we refer the customer to someone else.

"I really like this store and I enjoy what I do. But being a store manager, even in a health food store, can lend itself to stress. You have employees underneath you, an owner above you, customers, all kinds of sales people, and you're being pulled in a lot of different directions. You need a lot of patience, a lot of love."

How Theresa Got Started

"I've been into a more healthy lifestyle for a lot of years, but I had no idea I'd end up in a health food store and really like it. I was unemployed back in 1990 and knowing very little about health food stores or the health food industry itself, I walked into a place that was being built. I got the job that same day. Ever since then, I've been led in this direction.

"I had a sales background and some skills but very little training, so I learned on the job. You'll find that a lot of people learn on the job in the health food industry. Unless you're going to school to learn about health and nutrition, you end up being self-taught.

"To me this is a way of life. The more people who know about organic food and health, the healthier we will be as a society as a whole. The more farmers who grow organic and the more people who buy organic, the sooner prices will go down and products will be more readily available. Then more people can be turned on to this way of life.

"I know people who have gone from doctors and pills and medication and have changed their lifestyle and now no longer need the doctors and pills and medication. I'm not downgrading traditional medicine; there are many people who have been helped that way. But there are alternatives, and if we begin to look at them and if the holistic professionals and the doctors begin to work with each other as opposed to against each other, we can change lives."

Getting That Job

It's been Theresa's experience that many health food stores are very open to training new employees. At Cabbages they look for certain qualities in job candidates. "We want to see a good attitude, a strong interest and willingness to learn," Theresa says. "It's usually obvious when you interview someone, when you talk to them."

Theresa suggests that, in addition to scanning help wanted ads, job seekers should stop by the stores where they would like to work. "At Cabbages we don't advertise when we have an opening," Theresa explains. "We would put a sign in the window or check around through word of mouth."

Salaries in Health Food Stores

Entry-level salaries usually are quite low, from $5 to $6 an hour, depending on your knowledge and skills and the area of the country in which you work. As you climb up the ladder, the pay scale doesn't necessarily climb with you. "The health food business doesn't pay very well," says Theresa, "but you don't do it for the money. You're in the health food business to be in the health food business."

Restaurants

Scattered throughout the country are hundreds of restaurants catering to people who prefer to eat healthful as well as tasty food. Health nuts can find satisfying careers in these settings, working as food servers, menu planners, or chefs and cooks.

Moosewood Restaurant

Moosewood Restaurant, in Ithaca, New York, opened its doors in 1973 as a collectively run vegetarian eating establishment. Part of the counterculture at the time, Moosewood workers were early adherents to the now popular philosophy that food could be healthful and taste good at the same time. They also felt that the workplace should be a fun place to be, with all business decisions made jointly.

At present, eighteen women and men rotate through the jobs necessary to make a restaurant go, planning menus, setting long-term goals—and washing pots. Their ranks are bolstered by about half a dozen employees.

Most of the Moosewood collective have worked together for over ten years, several since the restaurant's early days.

Moosewood was at first known only locally. Now, two decades and several highly acclaimed cookbooks later, Moosewood's reputation for serving fine food in a friendly atmosphere has spread nationally.

And they have not lost sight of their original philosophy. They are still owned and run collectively, and they still serve quality meals at reasonable prices.

David Hirsch, Natural Foods Chef

David Hirsch joined the Moosewood collective in 1976. He started as a waiter/busboy but soon took on the responsibilities of chef and menu planner. He is also the author of *The Moosewood Restaurant Kitchen Garden* and co-author of three others—*New Recipes from Moosewood Restaurant, Sundays at Moosewood Restaurant,* and *Moosewood Restaurant Cooks at Home.*

David earned his Bachelor of Architecture degree in 1968 at City College of New York. He worked in various architectural firms for a few years before moving to Ithaca.

David talks about how it all started: "My desire to leave the city and join the back-to-the-land movement brought me to Ithaca in 1972. I spent a couple of years building a house in the country, then to earn some money, I got a job as a cook for a couple of different fraternities at Cornell University. I could have summers off and could devote time to other pursuits. My interest in architecture was replaced with my love of the earth, gardening, hiking, and the out-of-doors.

"But I discovered I also loved to cook. It's fun and direct; the results are immediate.

"I got hooked up with Moosewood, by then in its third year, though at the time I wasn't thinking about a long-term career. I was disgruntled with the atmosphere cooking at the fraternities and wanted to be with people who shared my values. Moosewood was the perfect place."

Making a Collective Work

Collectives have come and gone over the years; it takes a lot of different elements to make one work. If this is a career path that intrigues you, these tips from David can point you in the right direction:

"To start a successful collective, just like with any business, you first must judge the need, do some market research. Are people clamoring for this business to serve them?

"Then you have to gather capital. Look for a guardian angel or a potential collective member with a trust fund!

"Banks are unlikely to immediately lend money to a business with no collateral. They might lend to individuals who can put up their homes, take a second mortgage—put their own capital on the line or that of a friend or relative. But banks are wary about putting their money down without having something to hold on to.

"With Moosewood an enormous amount of money wasn't necessary. We started with a small space and bought some second-hand equipment.

"Someone in the collective should also have some business background; if not, you need to be prepared to hire someone who does.

"Specifically in the restaurant business, you need to be able to work under pressure. So many restaurants go under. Moosewood has been around all these years because we continue to look for interesting international recipes that please our customers. And our timing was right.

"And, obviously, in a worker/manager situation, you need to be somehow connected to other people who have similar interests. You can't do it yourself. You need good support, a network of people you trust. We didn't put an ad in the paper looking for collective members. Moosewood is unique, a network of connected friends and acquaintances that grew in a fairly organic way.

"Twenty years ago the times were different. But a collective is still a possibility—if the variables can be jelled. Employees can be the owners of their businesses. In fact, there are stories coming from everywhere about employers selling their businesses back to the employees.

"Once you are involved, try to create situations that can expand your interest in whatever you want to do so it doesn't get stale.

"Look for something that really excites you, interests you. You have to be comfortable with it. If you find yourself watching the clock, wishing you were out of there, then you really probably should be out of there.

"Being a part of a collective involves commitment. With a more traditional job, you can just go home at the end of the day. With a collective there are meetings to attend and responsibilities to share. You have to be willing to do that."

Getting a Foot in the Door

"We occasionally take on new members. To be a part of Moosewood, we'd have to see a resume, but we tend to hire people we can interview on a personal basis. We work very closely together in a small space.

"Write first, then if we like what we see, you'd need to come up to Ithaca.

"To get a foot in the door, it's a good idea to take a few cooking courses, though there are not very many that specialize in just vegetarian cuisine. Various culinary institutes or some community colleges or adult education programs might offer appropriate courses.

"At Moosewood, nobody starts off right away as a chef. You need to gain some experience here, to have the repertoire down.

"We start our new members off slowly, working with someone more senior at the beginning, as an extra cook on a shift.

"And, of course, we also have recipes written down to follow."

You can write to Moosewood for more information at

Moosewood Restaurant
215 North Cayuga Street
Ithaca, NY 14850

David's Duties at Moosewood

David divides his time between cooking, planning menus, ordering food and supplies, testing recipes for the books, writing, attending meetings, and occasionally waiting on tables.

Because of the Moosewood cookbooks, he also occasionally is involved in book promotions, attending local book signings, or appearing on television and radio shows. He also does some catering and consulting and teaches hands-on cooking workshops.

The Finances Involved

"At Moosewood, our priorities have always had a lot to do with how we feel about the workplace and not about amassing great fortunes. With so many people involved sharing dividends, income gets watered down, even with a large book advance.

"The reasons to be in our collective have to be heartfelt. Rewards could be strongly financial in another type of collective or business venture, but not necessarily so. It depends on the market, where you are, what service or product you are providing.

"In a restaurant collective, financial rewards are far from glamorous. Entry-level salaries start somewhere in the teens. With three or four years of experience someone might make $20,000 or so, depending on how many hours a week he or she chooses to work."

The Hours Involved

"Most traditional restaurant owners would probably have to work sixty to seventy hours a week. One advantage of a collective is you can work fewer hours if you choose."

The Upside

"From the very beginning I really liked Moosewood. It felt different to me from any other job. There's no hierarchy, you're

working with peers. There are built-in checks and balances—
no authority figures to say 'you have to do it this way because I
say so.' Everyone's on equal ground.

"The atmosphere is supportive rather than competitive. You
don't have a group of people vying for a vice presidency or the
next upper position.

"There's a more honest approach on a daily basis. It's all very
appealing, direct. You go in, make the food, and people appreciate it. This is something I can care about. I feel good about
what I'm doing."

The Downside

"What I like least is dealing with the push and pull from all the
different directions, the different people. The collective process working towards consensus can be frustrating at times."

You can read more about David Hirsch and writing cookbooks in Chapter Six.

Steve Herrell, Founder of Steve's Ice Cream

You might be wondering why a section on ice cream, especially
Steve's Ice Cream, is turning up in a book on careers for health
nuts. What's so healthful about all that fat? Right?

Well, twenty or so years ago, the first Steve's Ice Cream was
a groundbreaker in a movement that brought people back to a
more natural way of enjoying ice cream. Its founder, Steve
Herrell, wanted to start a fun business and he thought ice cream
would be just the thing.

Steve talks about how he got started: "Ice cream has been
around commercially for 140 years or so, and in the old days it
was very good. But it started declining in quality. Around 1973
it had gotten about as low as it could get. At that time there
seemed to be a sudden revelation that ice cream could be a lot
better than what we'd been getting. There was a whole movement to go back to the basics then, in food and other areas.

That's when natural food stores started, vegetarian restaurants, granola—the timing was right.

"I remembered our days at home when I was growing up, making ice cream in the backyard with the family. My dad and my great uncle taught us all how to make it. We learned about the fun of everyone taking a turn at the crank, and the antici-pation when putting in the ice and salt and the great moment when it was done and opening it up and taking out the dasher.

"I'm a certified high school English teacher in Massachusetts. I had done a little of that but found it was not my cup of tea. I drove a taxi for a couple of years while trying to figure out what I would do with the remainder of my life. I knew it would not be taxi driving. The main thing I knew I wanted to do was run my own business and be in charge. And it was a somewhat sec-ondary question just what that business might be."

Steve opened Steve's Ice Cream on Elm Street in Somerville, Massachusetts, on a Friday in June, 1973. Within the first three days he had a full crowd every night. He spent about $200 to advertise on WBCN, a popular radio station in Boston, but it was word of mouth that packed the place. The local press paid Steve's a lot of attention and articles started appearing regu-larly in the *Boston Globe*. Not too much later came national recognition. The *New Yorker* was the first; it showcased Steve's Ice Cream in the "Talk of the Town" section.

Steve's Ice Cream was the first parlor to make its own ice cream in full view of all the customers. Steve was also the first to popularize using "Mix-ins," which is now a trademark for the crushed up Heath bars, Oreo cookies, M&M's and all those other goodies you can blend in with your ice cream. Today it is commonplace, but then it was pure novelty.

"I thought it would be a fun business," Steve explains, "an interesting thing to watch, making ice cream in full view on the premises. This was a business concept. I wanted it to be an active kind of a place, a place of function where something would be going on. We had a player piano, colorful pictures on the walls; there was a certain personal atmosphere to the place.

"I earned a B.A. in sociology and I think, though, that if I had gone to business school and earned a business degree I would not have done Steve's. Part of its attraction and charm was due to my obvious lack of business training. I was not following any kind of mold—it was a pure vision of what I thought it could be and how it should operate. If I had gone to business school I might have been taught it wouldn't work.

"I started with almost nothing. I used what personal savings I had and credit cards. It wasn't nearly enough, but because of that it was a very personal kind of place. For example, the chairs and tables didn't match. Normally when opening a restaurant, you'd go out and buy twelve tables and chairs that were all the same. But I went to used furniture stores and picked out two chairs here, three there and painted them (orange, red, and purple.) You wouldn't learn that in a business course.

"Also, there were generally no books then on how to make ice cream with an ice and salt freezer. In fact, the freezer I bought to use there went too fast. The motor moved the dasher too rapidly and it didn't mimic the action of a hand crank as I thought it would. But it was a little late at that point—I was due to open in three days. It was pure panic. I took the motor off and put on a gear reducer, which essentially slowed the whole thing down.

"We sold out almost every night. I opened with just one or two employees and I was making all of the ice cream and staying up every night to do it. I was very happy that it was so successful and so well received right away, but then I had to close for about two weeks to reorganize, to move in more equipment and hire more staff and train them to make ice cream. When I first opened I didn't even have enough refrigeration space."

Steve attributes his success to a variety of reasons.

"I never advertised that the ice cream was all natural, but people just picked that up and assumed it. My hope was to take cream and eggs and sugar and mix it up, flavor it, and freeze it.

But health codes don't allow you do just that in a retail situation. You need to use a pre-packaged mixture made by a dairy processor under controlled conditions. The mixture's main ingredients are cream and sugar and it's homogenized and pasteurized—the pasteurization is an important part of the process. It also has stabilizers to prevent ice crystals from forming during temperature fluctuation and to give the ice cream body and not let it melt too fast.

"It doesn't have preservatives to make it last longer as you'd find in bread, for example, but it does have additives. The air content in my ice cream is very low, though, which means it tastes richer and you get more substance per teaspoon than in a high air content ice cream.

"Basically, the ice cream tastes great. I do my own flavoring, and that's all natural. I don't go for weird, I go for good. The flavors are unique, such as root beer or Earl Grey tea. Then there's malted vanilla, pure vanilla, pure chocolate, real strawberries in the strawberry.

"The idea of making the ice cream on the premises was unique, the Mix-ins, and the store itself all contributed to the success. There was a real character to it. It wasn't a big impersonal chain then and people could sense that there was a real person behind the whole thing. People related to that and liked it."

The Finances Involved

Usually with a new business you can't expect to break even or show a profit the first year or so, but that wasn't the case with Steve's. "I always had enough to live on and there was always a high volume of customers. The problem with Steve's was that the prices weren't high enough so it always seemed like there wasn't enough money. So I raised the prices and worried that the customers wouldn't want to come, but there was never any negative feedback. All through my four years there my prices should have been at least 25 percent higher than they were.

"I sold Steve's in August of '77, all assets and liabilities. There was a nice difference between my initial investment and the final sale price. The only thing I kept was the player piano. Two brothers and a third partner bought Steve's and expanded it a bit before selling it to a company called Integrated Resources, which then sold it to another partnership. I have no involvement with any of the Steve's you see around the country. The ice cream at Steve's is very different now and it's not made on site anymore. The original character has been diluted, which is what tends to happen with a chain.

"I had a three-year noncompetition agreement with the people I sold to. It expired in August of 1980. In September of 1980 I opened Herrell's Ice Cream in Northampton, about ninety miles west of Boston where Mount Holyoke and Smith Colleges are.

"Very soon after that I became interested in expanding and enlisted the services of a franchise consultant. I then opened the first Herrell's franchise store in Harvard Square on Dunster Street in '82. It's still there and they use all my formulas and trademarks. At this time, there are two other franchises in Boston as well as an ice cream bon bon plant.

"But Herrell's has a very non-chain feel to it," Steve says. He used that old player piano for awhile at Herrell's but these days it's sitting in storage. "The customers would play the same songs over and over—Rubber Ducky (a favorite of the Smithies), Maple Leaf Rag, William Tell Overture, The Entertainer Rag—and drive the staff crazy. We have about 1,200 square feet, decorated with Caribbean colors, greens and reds, a tin ceiling and two giant stuffed bears sitting in the window having a dish of vanilla ice cream."

Steve has twenty-five employees and he puts in about thirty-five hours a week at Herrell's. He's at the point where he could let employees handle the day-to-day tasks, but he still prefers to keep his hand in. "I could be semi-retired now, but then I would start to lose touch with what's going on; you don't hear feedback from customers and everything would be second hand. I always appreciate when customers come up and tell me how much they enjoy Herrell's, and lots of people come up to me who remember going to the Somerville store twenty years ago, standing in line, and having that unique ice cream experience."

Some Words of Advice

Steve says you should just go ahead and follow your vision— and don't go to business school. "I would have been more fearful if I had known what problems might have come up. If you get too much advice you could be overwhelmed. I could make a list of all the potential problems and publish it, but it wouldn't be a good idea. Your creativity would get squelched."

For more information about Herrell's Ice Cream franchises you can contact Steve at

Herrell's
8 Old South Street
Northampton, MA 01060

Diet And Nutrition

It seems fitting that, after talking about ice cream and all that unmentionable fat, we go on to discuss the field of diet and nutrition.

Health nuts interested in this specialization find employment as dietitians or nutritionists in hospitals, schools, day care centers, summer camps, hotels, natural food stores, and weight-loss clinics. They can also set themselves up in private practice.

Historically, dietitians have been thought of as the professionals who work in hospitals. Nutritionists are thought of more as working in the community on an outpatient basis, counseling for nutritional problems or weight loss. They also work in health food stores, helping customers with nutritional concerns.

But basically, the two terms carry the same weight, as long as both professionals have gone through similar training programs and are licensed by the state. Now and again, you might run across someone who claims the title nutritionist but doesn't have the proper qualifications and license to do so.

The Role of Registered Dietitians and Nutritionists

There are several different kinds of dietitians with a wide variety of duties.

CLINICAL DIETITIANS generally work in a hospital setting in a patient-oriented role. Each dietitian is usually assigned one or two floors, about fifty patients per dietitian.

Clinical dietitians visit patients, review their medical records, and evaluate their nutritional status to determine what would be the best diet for them to be on given their specific medical problems. They would look at the chart to see what the patients were admitted for and what kind of lab results they had. They would interview the patients, asking about their diet history, what they usually eat, if they've been following any special diets, if they've lost weight recently, if they have any trouble swallowing, chewing, and so forth.

That information is then recorded in the medical record before it gets processed in the diet office where the menus originate. Afterward, it is passed to the kitchen so patients can be fed appropriate meals three times a day.

Dietitians work with regular diets or design diets with restrictions for patients with ailments such as diabetes, renal or cardiac problems, or cancer.

SPECIALIZED DIETITIANS work with special-needs patients such as those in kidney dialysis centers where diet plays a major role in the treatment of the patient. They deal with tube feedings or parenteral nutrition, when a patient is fed a concentrated formula of carbohydrates and protein through a large vein.

ADMINISTRATIVE DIETITIANS oversee the entire food service operation from purchasing, storing, and preparing food and other functions of the kitchen.

COMMUNITY DIETITIANS or nutritionists work with patients on an outpatient basis, in health food stores, clinics, or private practice. They counsel patients to help them lose weight, bring down their cholesterol levels, deal with food allergies, or handle a variety of other concerns.

DIETETIC TECHNICIANS Registered dietitians, especially in large and busy hospitals, depend on the help of registered dietetic technicians, or diet techs, as they are called. Most diet techs are clinically oriented and do basic screenings of patients, review medical records, and document their findings on the patient charts. They generally handle the less complicated cases, leaving specialized patient needs to registered dietitians.

Diet techs can also work in nursing homes, overseeing the food service operation or working in the kitchen.

DIET AIDES/NUTRITION ASSISTANTS Diet aides function in a clerical role. They write the patient's name and room number on the menus, pass menus out to the patients on the floors, and wait while the different preferences are checked. They then review the menus, making sure they've been marked properly.

Training for Dietitians

A dietitian must have a four-year degree in foods and nutrition from an accredited university. Course work will cover a lot of science—biology, chemistry, physiology—as well as nutrition, math, foods, and food science.

A six- to nine-month supervised internship is also required. Some programs allow the internship to run concurrently with the senior year; in other programs the internship can be started only after graduation.

After the internship you are eligible to take a registration exam administered by the American Dietetic Association, the national professional organization. After passing the exam, you are then a registered dietitian.

Some dietitians go on for a master's degree, especially if they are interested in administrative positions or want to maintain their competitiveness for jobs.

Training for Diet Techs

Diet techs usually earn a two-year degree in foods and nutrition at a community college. They are then eligible to take an exam administered by the American Dietetic Association to become a registered dietetic technician. Many then find jobs and continue to study on the weekends to earn their four-year degrees.

Training for Diet Aides

Diet aides and nutrition assistants usually have no formal training in foods and nutrition. They must have a high school diploma and have good written and verbal skills. The work is mainly clerical and most are trained on the job.

Becoming a diet aide is a good way to get a taste for the profession, so to speak. After spending some time in a hospital food department, you can then decide if you want to go on for further training.

The Hours You'll Work

Your shifts will vary depending upon the setting, but for the most part dietitians avoid weekend work and the late night and overnight shifts that many nurses must deal with. But some dietitians are on call over the weekend and must come in for emergencies.

Diet techs and assistants aren't as lucky, and generally they pull regular weekend duty.

For diet aides, the earliest shift would start about 5:30 in the morning in order to help serve breakfast. They would finish up about 2:30 in the afternoon. The latest shift would finish at about 7:30 in the evening after the dinner meal is over.

Salaries for Dietitians, Diet Techs, and Assistants

As with most professions, salaries vary depending upon the region of the country in which you work and the size of the hiring institution's budget. Registered dietitians usually are paid an annual salary. For entry-level candidates, that could begin in the mid twenties and increase with more experience.

Administrators, depending upon their responsibilities, could earn from $30,000 to $80,000 a year.

Diet techs generally start in the low twenties. Diet aides are usually paid hourly, from $5.50 to $7.

The benefits of working in a hospital usually make up for the low pay. This includes good health care plans, pensions, vacation days, sick leave, holidays, and personal days.

Emily Friedland, Dietitian

Emily Friedland is the assistant director of food and nutrition at Boca Raton Community Hospital in Boca Raton, Florida. She has a B.S. in nutrition and foods from Cornell University and an M.A. in food service management from New York University.

Emily talks about her job: "I am responsible for the entire department; we have about one hundred employees. Our department is made up of different sections—patient feeding, cafeteria feeding, visitor coffee shop, and clinical nutrition. In the clinical nutrition area I directly supervise a total of twenty-five dietitians, diet techs, and nutrition aides.

"I review their work, maintain and update a diet manual, which is all the different diets our patients might be on, and write and implement policies and procedures. My job is varied; it's different each day. We have an in-service training program, so every month there are one or two classes we present, and we are continually measuring the quality of our performance.

"I enjoy being in a management position. You never know what you're going to face when you walk in the door in the morning. There are always different crises that come up—a piece of equipment is broken, or someone didn't show up to work. In the food service industry you are committed to getting those three meals out every day, and if someone doesn't show up, you can't just say, 'Well, we're short-handed so we won't serve breakfast today.' You have to put out a product no matter what the inputs are.

"There's a lot of variety. There are always new cases, different needs—it doesn't get boring.

"I just wish we had more respect in the health care industry. But I think it's coming. The stereotype of the gray-haired lady in the school cafeteria is changing. People are recognizing that nutrition does have a great influence on health—treatment of disease and also prevention of disease.

"And the training is changing too. It's more clinically oriented. Things that the dietitian was doing eighteen, twenty years ago when I first started are what the diet tech does now. The registered dietitian is getting more involved in the complicated cases now. As our dietitians are being more and more specialty trained and the physicians see that this person really knows what he or she is talking about, there will be more and more respect.

"We're also lobbying very hard to have our services covered in the new health care reform. Right now nutrition services are not covered by insurance programs and sometimes people are reluctant to spend $60 or whatever to consult a dietitian. But on the other hand, they'll go into a health food store and spend hundreds of dollars on vitamins they don't need and that are only going to go right through their systems. They'll pay for that but they won't pay for a licensed practitioner to really put them straight as far as what they need to be doing.

"And I don't think for the amount of education and training we have that we are recognized and compensated as much as some of the other health care professionals.

"But the upside is it's a great job if you enjoy working in a health care setting, working with people, but don't want to do hands-on care. And if you enjoy the relationship between food and health, you're able to put that into practice."

How Emily Got Started

Emily has been working in the field for twenty years. "In high school I always enjoyed home economics and I had a teacher who introduced me to the field. I didn't start out as a nutrition major. I was a little scared off by all the science requirement. But I did take a nutrition class my first semester at college and decided that I really liked it and quickly changed my major from consumer economics to foods and nutrition.

"I also worked in a nursing home in a kitchen as a food service worker during summers while in college.

"I'd advise anyone wanting to pursue this career to go ahead and get the proper education and training. You can start out as a diet tech through a two-year program to see if it's what you'd like, and then go on for your bachelor's degree."

Health Inspectors

In the world of food there are growers, preparers, servers, sales people, and dietary and nutritional consultants. But there are a few other food-related careers that could appeal to health nuts. To ensure that food handlers meet certain health and safety standards, local, state, and federal government agencies and a few private-sector concerns such as hospitals and manufacturing firms employ a variety of inspectors.

Health inspectors work with engineers, chemists, microbiologists, health workers, and lawyers to ensure compliance with public health and safety regulations governing food, drugs, cosmetics, and other consumer products. These are the major types of inspector positions that would interest health nuts:

FOOD INSPECTORS inspect meat, poultry, and their byproducts to ensure they are safe for public use. They observe slaughtering, processing, and packaging operations and check for product labeling and proper sanitation.

CONSUMER SAFETY INSPECTORS specialize in food, feeds, pesticides, weights and measures, cosmetics, drugs, and medical equipment. Some are proficient in more than one specialization. Working individually or in teams, they periodically check firms that produce, handle, store, and market the products they regulate. They look for inaccurate labeling or chemical or bacteriological contamination that could result in a product becoming harmful to health.

AGRICULTURAL QUARANTINE INSPECTORS protect American agriculture from the spread of foreign plant and animal pests and diseases. They inspect ships, airplanes, trains, and motor vehicles entering the United States, looking for restricted or prohibited plants, animals, insects, agricultural commodities, and animal by-products.

AGRICULTURAL COMMODITY GRADERS apply quality standards to ensure that retailers and consumers know the quality of the products they purchase. They inspect eggs, meat, poultry, fruit and vegetables, grain, tobacco, cotton, or dairy products. After determining quality and grade, they issue official grading certificates.

Environmental Health Inspectors ensure that food, water, and air meet government standards. They may specialize in dairy products, food sanitation, waste control, air or water pollution, institutional sanitation, or occupational health. They check the safety and cleanliness of food produced in dairies and processing plants, or served in restaurants, hospitals, and other institutions.

To read more about careers related to the environment, see Chapter Seven.

Training for Inspectors

Because of the variety of inspector positions, the education and training requirements also vary. In general, an inspector is expected to have a combination of education and experience. College programs should include related courses. Job candidates often must take written examinations before being considered for employment.

Salaries for Inspectors

According to a 1992 study conducted by the U.S. Office of Personnel Management, average annual salaries for a few selected inspector positions are as follows:

Mine safety and health inspectors	$48,400
Environmental protection specialists	$45,700
Import specialists	$43,600
Safety and occupational health managers	$43,400
Alcohol, tobacco, and firearms inspectors	$41,500

Public health quarantine inspectors	$39,600
Customs inspectors	$36,400
Agricultural commodity graders	$34,200
Food inspectors	$29,800
Consumer safety inspectors	$27,600
Environmental protection assistants	$24,800

Getting That Job

Employment for inspectors is expected to increase faster than the average for all occupations throughout the year 2005, reflecting growing public demand for a safe environment and quality products.

Information on jobs with the federal government is available from offices of the state employment service, area offices of the U.S. Office of Personnel Management, and Federal Job Information Centers in large cities throughout the country. For information on jobs as specific inspectors, you may also contact the federal department or agency that employs them.

Information about state and local government jobs is usually available from state civil service commissions, usually located in each state capital, or from local government offices.

Information about jobs in the private sector is available from the state employment service, listed in your telephone directory.

CHAPTER SIX

The Health Beat

Writing and Reporting on Health Issues

Health nuts who combine their knowledge and love of good health, food, fitness, and a clean environment with a talent for writing can bring in extra income or land themselves a full-time career. With a thorough grasp of your subject, an understanding of the needs of book publishers and magazine and newspaper editors—and a lot of drive and persistence—dedicated health nuts can teach others what they know through the written word.

Writing "How-To" and Self-Help Books

Investigate any bookstore or your local library and you'll find hundreds of volumes covering every aspect of the world of health, fitness, and medicine, from cooking and eating healthfully to spiritual and physical healing and a range of topics in between.

These "how-to" books can be very successful and publishers are always on the lookout for new projects that take a fresh approach. Here are just a few successful topics:

- Eating well

- Exercising

- Living well

- Psychology and relationships

- Recovery

- Reference

Deciding on a Topic

When deciding about what to write, it's a good idea to find a topic that hasn't been overdone. An overlooked subject, the results of new research, or a new slant or twist on an old subject can work; the trick is to find a hole in the marketplace, a gap that only your book can fill.

If you've come across a gap and thought of the perfect idea for a book to fill it, don't worry if you think your experience or knowledge is too limited. Very few writers can put together a book without doing research or interviewing experts in the field. Professional associations can direct you to members who would be willing to help.

Getting Started

After you've developed your idea and have checked to make sure it brings something new to the market, you need to prepare a book proposal. Your proposal will state your topic, why your book has something different to offer, who will buy your book, and what format your book will take. You'll need a table of contents, a sample chapter or two, and an outline of the remaining chapters. An excellent resource to guide you is Michael Larsen's book, *How to Write a Book Proposal* (Writer's Digest Books.) In addition to explaining the proper format and content for a book proposal, it also helps you decide if your idea is a viable one.

What to Do with Your Book Proposal

While you study the variety of titles already out there, take note of the particular publishing houses that had put them in print. Your book proposal has to be sent to publishers who handle your topic. You can write to the various publishers for their catalogs; this will give you an idea of their full range and will show you where your title might fit their list. You can also study the *Writer's Market* (Writers Digest Books), an annual guide that lists publishers and their needs and requirements.

Some writers prefer to concentrate on their writing (and related health interests) and they work with agents who handle the selling side. Finding an agent can take almost as much time as finding a publisher, but in the end, it is well worth the effort. A good agent knows what projects will fit with which publishers—and which will not. You can find an agent through *The Literary Marketplace* (R.R. Bowker), available at your library, or through *Writer's Digest's Guide to Literary Agents & Art/ Photo Reps*. You can also write to the Association of Authors' Representatives (AAR, 10 Astor Place, Third Floor, New York, NY 10003) for a list of its member agents. AAR members agree to adhere to a specific code of ethics; the AAR's list, however, does not specify areas of interest.

What Happens Next?

Once your proposal has been submitted to a publisher, the waiting begins. If your project grabs the right editor's interest, if you've presented your subject well and have made a convincing argument for the viability of your project—and you've been lucky—you might be asked to submit the completed manuscript for consideration. The best-case scenario would be an acceptance based upon your proposal. Successful writers know that there are two keys to joining the ranks of published authors:

1. An interesting and well-executed manuscript/proposal, and

2. Persistence.

If your idea is a good one, the quality of your work is exceptional, and you don't give up easily, approaching a publisher can eventually pay off.

David Hirsch, Gardener, Chef, and Author

David Hirsch has been with Moosewood Restaurant, a collectively run vegetarian eating establishment in Ithaca, New York, for almost twenty years. (David and Moosewood are profiled in Chapter Five.)

David collaborated with other collective members to write *New Recipes from Moosewood Restaurant, Sundays at Moosewood Restaurant,* and *Moosewood Restaurant Cooks at Home.*

David is also the author of *The Moosewood Restaurant Kitchen Garden,* a practical guide to creative gardening for the adventurous cook. While sharing his personal experiences with the reader, David gives instructions for growing and harvesting, creating garden design plans, and using more than thirty vegetables and thirty-five herbs, including edible flowers and gourmet vegetables. Also included is a chapter of recipes that puts your garden's yield to good use. The book has been well received, with more than fifty thousand copies in print.

David talks about his book and how he got started: "Even when I was a kid growing up in Bayside, Queens, we had this little postage-stamp garden in front of the house and I used to plant seeds and water them. I wasn't an adventurous gardener then, but I enjoyed it and I had that sense of continuity, of taking care of something.

"For me there was always a very strong connection between the process of growing and cooking, and these are two areas that strongly interest me. I love to garden and I love to cook. It seemed as if it would be a very enjoyable project, to take two things I cared about and knew a fair amount about and write about them.

"We already had literary agents because of the other Moosewood books and they suggested I write a proposal. I put it together and they submitted it to Simon & Schuster.

"It's always nice to make money at something you love, but as with any job, there are always some stresses or concerns. For me, there was certainly the concern of writing a whole book by myself. But I did get a lot of support. Other Moosewood people helped out and tested my recipes. Writing requires a real commitment of time and space to get it done. You have deadlines hanging over your head all the way through. The publishers want half the manuscript by a certain date, the remaining half by another date. Then you send it in and they send it back to you with suggestions for changes and another deadline they want to receive everything by. So you have to set up that discipline in your life.

"A lot of people who aren't full-time writers are doing something else with their time. You have to work around that, to fit everything in."

Some Advice from David

"Pick an area that interests you, an area you want to learn more about, because with most writing projects you have to do some research. You need to know something about the subject; you need to have something to say.

"In terms of marketing, what you have to say should have some angle that's different from what's already out there. There must be hundreds of cookbooks on the market. What a writer has to do is take a unique perspective and work with that."

Writing Articles for Magazines and Newspapers

For those of you who feel tackling a book-length project seems too overwhelming, at least at first, you can always start with magazine and newspaper articles. There are hundreds of magazines that, if not entirely devoted to health and fitness, include some kind of health or lifestyle articles for their readership. Take a look at any good-size newsstand; make note of health and fitness magazines, then flip through other general-interest publications to see which ones also include articles on the same subjects.

The *Writer's Market*, in addition to listing book publishers and their requirements, also contains a hefty selection of both trade and consumer publications.

Most major newspapers and many local ones have health or lifestyle sections or columns. Although these are often written by full-time staffers, many newspapers are open to free-lance submissions. You can find a listing of newspapers in your library. Abalone Press has compiled a computerized directory on disk of the nation's biggest dailies, complete with the names of nearly two thousand key editors. It is formatted to work with whatever word processing or data base program you use, and it can save you hours of unnecessary typing while sending out multiple submissions. For more information you can contact Abalone Press at 14 Hickory Avenue, Takoma Park, MD 20912.

How to Get Started Free-lancing

You don't have to work full-time for a publication to write health-related articles; most magazines use a good number of free-lance submissions each month. Most free-lancers work as independent contractors, setting up a home office, sending out article ideas or completed manuscripts, negotiating payment, and setting their own hours. Of course, there are deadlines to meet and a publishable standard of work to deliver.

Editors want to see well-written, informative articles that will be of interest to their readers. A good article should have a strong lead and a body filled with examples, anecdotes, and quotes from experts.

How Much You'll Be Paid

Payment for one article varies from publication to publication but could range from $50 or so for small magazines to $200 or

$300 and up to $1000 or more for national magazines. Some magazines pay you as soon as they've accepted your manuscript; others wait until your article has been published.

The trick to making enough money is to allow one article to bring in more than one fee. As long as the publications do not have a competing circulation, and you haven't sold all rights to the article, you can place your work more than once. For example, an article on healthful cooking could find homes in several regional magazines, as well as with local newspapers.

Reslanting an article to capture a broader audience can also help increase your salary. An article for a children's magazine on how to eat well can be rewritten to address an adult audience. Reslanting increases the number of publications you can approach; resales increase your paycheck.

Approaching Editors

There are different ways to approach a publication; the method you choose should follow the preferences the editors have expressed in the various market books or in their own guidelines for writers. To get a copy of a magazine's guidelines, send your request with an SASE (self-addressed stamped envelope).

It is also a good idea to have read the magazine for which you would like to write so you are familiar with its format and style. If you can't find the magazine at a newsstand, you can write to the publishers for a sample copy.

The first rule when approaching a magazine is to make sure your letter is addressed to a specific editor by name. You can find this information in the magazine's masthead or listed in the *Writer's Market*.

Some editors don't want to see an entire article right away; they would rather you send them a query letter. A query letter is a mini proposal, stating the topic about which you would like to write, how you would approach it, and what qualifies you to write it. The query letter gives the editor an idea of your writing style and helps him or her decide quickly if the subject matter is right for the publication. You might be proposing an article the magazine has already covered or has plans to cover with a different writer. Query letters save everyone time.

If an editor likes your query, you'll probably receive a letter asking to see the completed manuscript. New free-lancers just breaking in often have to write the article "on spec" with no guarantee of publication. Once you have some publishing credits under your belt, a query letter can lead to a paid assignment.

Other editors will bypass the query stage and ask to see the entire manuscript first.

Once your piece has been accepted, be prepared to wait several months before it sees print, although newspapers usually have a faster turn around time than magazines.

Some Sample Markets

In addition to a wide variety of national magazines that cover everything from tofu to tennis elbow, most states have regional magazines with health or lifestyle features. The following is a small sampling of publications that accept articles health nuts would enjoy writing:

American Health has three departments open to free-lance writers: profiles of noted people in the health care field; first-person pieces about deeply felt personal experiences; and opinion pieces on timely or controversial health care issues. Payment is one dollar per word on acceptance. Profiles run 1,500 to 2,500 words, and articles start at 750 words on up. Send articles to 28 West 23rd Street, New York, NY 10010.

Jenny Craig's Your Body, Your Health is an all-purpose women's health and fitness magazine. It features stories on weight control, nutrition, exercise, and general health. "No disease-of-the-month stories," the editor says. "Our focus is wellness. We are for the healthy person who wants to stay well." Payment is fifty to seventy cents a word. Department pieces run from 250 to 700 words; features run up to 2,000 words. Send your query letter and clips (copies of your previously published articles) to 1633 Broadway, New York, NY 10019.

Men's Health publishes articles with a male slant, taking a broad view of health to cover both the physical and emotional. It includes profiles, exposés, and articles about relationships, eating right, and clinics that deal with specific health problems. Payment is twenty-five to sixty cents a word. Send submissions to Rodale Press, 33 East Minor Street, Emmaus, PA 18098.

Vegetarian Times uses articles with a vegetarian slant. It covers cooking, diet, lifestyle, health, consumer choices, natural foods, and environmental concerns. Payment is twenty cents a word upon acceptance. Send your query letter to Box 570, Oak Park, IL 60303.

Walking Magazine is a magazine for active people who understand their own bodies and how to develop them. Readers are 75 percent well-educated women, with a median age of forty. The editor wants articles on health, fitness, nutrition and food, and athletic gear and equipment. To approach this magazine, send a query letter that proposes your article idea and demonstrates your writing style. Payment is approximately seventy-five cents a word. Request guidelines or send submissions to 9-11 Harcourt Street, Boston, MA 02116.

Landing a Regular Column

Once you have established as a free-lancer, you can often land regular assignments with the same editors. This can even turn into a permanent column in a magazine or newspaper. And you can syndicate yourself, selling the same column to noncompeting newspapers across the country. Health columnists research and write about various topics of interest to their readers.

Nancy McVicar, Health Writer

Nancy McVicar is a senior writer at the *Sun-Sentinel*, a newspaper in Fort Lauderdale, Florida, with a circulation of about one million.

She works for the Lifestyle section, which has a health page every Thursday. Her stories also appear in other sections; recently a package of stories on the resurgence of infectious diseases began on the front cover.

Her articles focus on health, medicine, and fitness. Her work has been nominated for the Pulitzer Prize seven times, and several of her stories have won national awards.

Nancy talks about her job: "It's more than just medical writing because I've also been doing some stories on health care reform, which is another whole issue and that's taken up my time over the last couple of years. I try to explain the plan to readers so they can understand it, using actual people and their circumstances to tell the story. I look at questions such as why we need health care reform and what it means to the average person.

"Another story I recently did was about how antibiotics are losing their effectiveness because we're over-using them. I wouldn't call it breaking news; it's more a trend story. Here's something I think we need to be worried about, and why.

"In researching my stories I use a number of avenues. We have an electronic data base so I can ask our resource center here to do a search on what's been written in other publications about a particular subject.

"We can also get on the Information Superhighway, Internet, and make queries about things. I was preparing to do an interview with Kristine Gebbie, the AIDS czar appointed by Clinton, so I put out a question on the Internet asking people in the AIDS community what they would like to know from this woman. I got some really good suggestions for the interview.

"As it turned out, between the time I set it up and the time I actually did the interview, she resigned. It made an even better story about why she was quitting.

"For other sources, I talk to doctors and others in the medical community and I read a lot, particularly medical journals. I subscribe to *Journal of the American Medical Association* and the *New England Journal of Medicine* and I get probably half a dozen medical newsletters, from Johns Hopkins to the Mayo Clinic or the Lahey Clinic in Massachusetts. I also receive more consumer-oriented publications. *Consumer Reports* puts out a health letter and the Center for Science in the Public Interest has a couple of publications, including one on nutrition. They're the ones who broke the story on movie theater popcorn and how full of fat it is.

"I also get a lot of phone calls from interested readers who say, 'I wonder if you know anything about such and such,' or 'I read there's a new treatment for high blood pressure and what can you tell me about it?' If I get enough calls on a particular subject I might decide there's an interest here that needs to be addressed and start researching it and do a story about it.

"Every once in a while I do a question and answer column, when I think it's called for. Recently there was a case of hantavirus in Dade county. There had been an outbreak of it in the southwest last year and it killed about half the people who got it. It's a deadly virus and it turned up in South Dade. I did a Q and A to let readers know they didn't have to be too concerned, that it's not really contagious. You get it from breathing the dried-up urine of rodents that are infected.

"Finding ideas for stories is not my problem; finding time to do all the stories is the bigger problem. You can't do them in one afternoon. You have to use multiple sources. You have to call at least two or three experts, even though you might not end up quoting them all in the story. But you can never do a one-source medical story.

"We don't have a quota for the number of stories we're going to write. We don't do breaking stories that much. I'll take a whole list of stories to my editor and we discuss them and decide which we should do first. We work with the photo people and our graphic staff so we can illustrate them.

"I haven't been writing about fitness too much but we want to increase that; there's a big interest in it. One story that I did recently was an interview with a doctor who had given up medicine to become a fitness trainer. I got a lot of calls from people who wanted to contact him to hire him. There's a lot of interest in having a personal trainer. It's hard to figure out what you should be doing at the gym on your own.

"Other stories have an emotional aspect to them. Some of it is life and death, or the story I'm working on today is concerned with a new procedure for infertility that's allowing some men, who could never have fathered a child, to do that now.

"Another aspect to medical writing is investigative. You may have to start from scratch, search documents, knock on doors. An investigative story I did here was on HMOs and how well they treat their Medicare-age patients. People over sixty-five on Medicare have the option of joining an HMO, which is supposed to provide them with all the care they would get under Medicare, but for less money. As a writer, I was getting all sorts of complaints from people saying things like 'They let my husband die; they didn't send him to the specialist they should have.' There's money involved. The more care you give, the less money goes into the HMO's pocket, so there's a financial disincentive to give care. Two other people, cowriters and investigators, and I spent six months on an investigation. You can do it by yourself but it goes much faster if you have help. You may have to sift through tons of documents, which we did. We concluded that there were a lot of problems. Once we brought them to light, the federal government promised that they would fix them. They worked on it, but they haven't fixed anything yet. So my coworkers did another story, a follow-up, which brought more problems to light. And again, the government is promising to make changes to protect people's lives.

"It was a five-day series that went out over the wire services and got a lot of exposure. It also won a long list of awards for the three of us. It's gratifying to be a change agent. That's the whole point of an investigative piece, to get some change going."

Nancy was the first to break the story "Are your Cellular Telephones Safe?" She produced two or three articles on the topic. The stories went out over the wire and also ended up on "20/20" and "Sixty Minutes." The GAO (The General Accounting Office of the U.S. Government, which is also the investigative arm of Congress) was asked to do an in-depth report on whether or not cellular phones are safe, based on the stories Nancy wrote. The report has not yet been presented, but it's due out soon.

Nancy explains how she got involved: "I was doing a bigger piece on brain tumors and the latest treatment. In the course of doing this I kept hearing that some people were saying that their cellular phones had given them their brain tumors. My first reaction was 'yeah, right,' but then when I started investigating, I found out it could be true. There's no proof that it is, but even the phone companies have started putting disclaimers in their manuals saying don't hold this thing close to your head."

Nancy also did a piece on emergency rooms and how they are being used in place of the doctor's office for people who don't have insurance. "The point was that professionals who are trained to handle trauma are instead handling sore throats and sniffles. It was a mini-investigation. I spent time at two different hospitals observing what went on during the day and did a whole-page article with pictures that won a national award with a cash prize.

"There's so much out there to write about," Nancy says, "that you can really pick and choose what you're interested in or what you think your readers will be interested in. It's not as if next week I'm going to be writing the same old story about some council meeting.

"And there is a wealth of experts to talk to who are willing to give you their time. But you have to know enough to be able to ask the right questions. You have to background yourself a bit before you get a doctor on the phone. You want to be able to ask intelligent questions and not waste his or her time."

Getting Started as a Health and Medical Writer

Nancy McVicar says she sort of fell into witing about health. "I had done almost everything else on a newspaper and when this job was offered it sounded appealing. But a lot of people go into journalism initially and know they want to be medical writers. They can then pick their courses in school to get a good background.

"Take some combination of journalism and science and medicine courses. There are even some people who have gone to medical school. I think the *New York Times* has a medical writer who is an M.D., and ABC has Dr. Timothy Johnson.

"Salaries will vary. Small papers don't pay very much at all, and large papers can pay very well. If you're just starting, you could find yourself in the low to midtwenties range or less. But many small papers don't even necessarily have health and medical writers; they rely on the wire services to provide them with stories.

"With a few years' experience under your belt, you can move up the pay ladder to thirty or forty thousand. With several years at a large newspaper your salary could even be in the fifty thousand range.

"But most of the time, before you could be hired at a large newspaper, you'd have to have experience at a smaller one. You can start off doing general assignments before you move on to your plum position somewhere else."

Nancy's Background

Nancy always knew she wanted to be a writer, but she started out writing novels and poetry. "I still do that," Nancy says, "but not very much. You have to be able to make a living and you can do that as a reporter.

"I don't really have a medical background as such, but I do have a lot of medical people in my family and at one point I did entertain the thought of going into some kind of medical field myself. I've always had an interest in it and I think it helps." Nancy's first job came about as a result of a blind ad she answered for "someone with a good English background." The job turned out to be for an assistant to the society editor at a small paper in Kansas. She started out writing weddings and engagements and then branched out, doing features on her own, which were then published.

"I also was an editor for seven years," Nancy says. "I did enjoy it, but I chose to go back to writing because it's what I prefer. It's a lifestyle choice for me. I'd rather do the sleuthing that it takes to produce a story than deal with the nuts and bolts of going to meetings every day and editing other people's work. I prefer the writing; it's more creative.

"And with health writing, the job is never boring. Medicine is always changing; there's always something new."

Lecturers

Writers in the field of health can also supplement their income by taking to the lecture circuit. Once they've written a successful book, they are automatically considered experts on their subject, and these experts are usually in demand to speak in a variety of settings, such as bookstores, colleges and universities, and community centers.

Lecture tours usually are arranged in conjunction with the release of a book and become part of the publisher's promotional efforts. In this case, payment to the lecturer would be in the form of royalties, a percentage of the price for each book sold.

Other times, lecturers, either on their own or with the help of an agent or publicist, set up speaking engagements where an admission fee is charged. They are paid a set fee (which varies depending upon their popularity) or a percentage of the ticket receipts.

Successful lecturers generally have to be well-known figures with subjects that interest a wide audience.

Photographers

Writers who can take their own photographs can often increase the amount of money they'll be paid for an article. A photographer with writing and/or marketing skills—and a focused project—can set out on his or her own to capture images of the American health scene. Photographers take still shots or videos of workout routines and exercise programs and illustrate books and articles in hundreds of other ways.

A highly specialized field in photography that would interest some creative health nuts is food photography. Food photographers are responsible for all the beautiful photographs you see in cookbooks and magazines or in television commercials.

Training for Photographers

Some photographers are self-taught while others attend college or art school. Still others find a professional photographer with whom they can apprentice.

Photographers need to become familiar with all the technical as well as artistic aspects of photography. A part of any training program would include studying what other photographers produce.

Photographers with some market savvy also recognize the importance of acquiring good writing skills. This way they are able to write their own articles to go with their pictures, thus increasing their income.

Salaries for Photographers

Payment varies from assignment to assignment and from publication to publication. Sometimes a photographer will be paid a set amount for each photograph that eventually sees print. That amount will also vary depending on the size of the photograph—whether it fills a quarter, half, or full page. Photographs that make the cover of a magazine earn more.

Sometimes a photographer will work on an hourly or daily rate. An editor might agree to pay for two full days of work at a set fee. If the assignment takes longer, the photographer will not earn any more money for that particular job. At the same time, if he or she spends less time than originally planned, the editor does not expect a refund.

In addition to their fees, photographers usually are paid for any additional expenses such as travel and lodging or renting extra equipment or props.

CHAPTER SEVEN

Healing the Environment

H ealth nuts are concerned with more than just their own physical fitness and well-being. They realize that a healthy body and a healthy state of mind are possible only if the environment in which we all live is healthy, too. Some career titles that work toward that end include:

- Conservationists

- Educators

- Environmental Engineers

- Foresters

- Land Planners

- Landscape Architects and Designers

- Park Rangers

- Researchers

Working with the Land

The United States is filled with beautiful greenery, from the well-manicured lawns in suburban neighborhoods to public and private parks and forests. To design and maintain these areas, a growing number of residential, commercial, and government clients rely on the services of a wide range of horticulture, landscape, forest, and conservation specialists.

These specialists have the task of planning and caring for all kinds of land areas, paying attention to conservation and the impact on the environment as well as aesthetics.

Land Planners

Land planners work in urban or rural settings devising plans that best utilize a community's land. They are knowledgeable about zoning and building codes and environmental regulations. Before preparing plans for long-range development, land planners conduct detailed studies that show the current use. These reports include information concerning the location of streets, highways, water and sewer lines, public buildings, and recreational sites. This information allows them to propose ways of using undeveloped or underutilized land. Land planners then recommend layouts of buildings and other facilities such as subway lines and stations. Land planners also have to show how the plans will be carried out and what they will cost.

Land planners divide their time between office work and on-site inspections. They also attend meetings and public hearings with citizens' groups.

Employment for Land Planners

Two out of three land planners work for government planning agencies, from local cities and counties to state and federal agencies. Some of these agencies include the departments of Defense, Housing and Urban Development, and Transportation.

Other planners do consulting or work full-time for firms that provide services to private developers or government agencies. Private sector employers include management and public relations firms, architecture and surveying firms, educational institutions, and large land developers.

Salaries vary depending upon the hiring institution and the amount of education a land planner has pursued. Annual averages run $39,000 for bachelor's degree holders, $43,000 for those with master's degrees, and $57,000 for those with doctorates.

What It Takes to Be a Land Planner

Land planners, in addition to their training in planning, landscape architecture, and civil engineering, must also be diplomats with excellent communication skills. Land planners work and interact with a variety of related professionals, including architects, city managers, environmental engineers, and geographers. They must also be able to negotiate with groups who may oppose the proposed development.

Landscape Architecture

Landscape architecture is the design of outside areas that are beautiful, functional, and compatible with the natural environment. A landscape architect can work with small residential or commercial projects, or with complex projects on a much larger scale. These could include projects for cities or counties, industrial parks, historical sites, and a variety of other settings.

Training for Landscape Architects

A bachelor's or master's degree is usually necessary for entry into the profession. Many bachelor's of landscape architecture (B.L.A.) programs take five years to complete; a master's degree can take two or three years. The two-year master's program is designed for bachelor's-level landscape architects; the three-year program is for people with a bachelor's degree in a field other than landscape architecture.

Your college curriculum will include the following courses:

- History of Landscape Architecture
- Landscape Design and Construction
- Landscape Ecology
- Structural Design
- Drafting
- Urban and Regional Planning
- Design and Color Theory
- Soil Science
- Geology
- Meteorology
- Topography
- Plant Science and other introductory horticulture courses
- Civil Engineering, including grading and drainage and pipe design
- Construction Law and Contracts
- General Management

Going on for a master's degree will help refine your design abilities, focusing on more complex design problems. It also will add greatly to your employability and salary prospects.

Almost all of the fifty states require landscape architects to be licensed. Licensing is based on passing the Landscape Architect Registration Examination (LARE), sponsored by the Council of Landscape Architecture Registration Boards. Admission to the exam usually requires a college degree and from one to four years or more of work experience. Some states such as Florida and Arizona require an additional exam focusing on the laws or plant materials indigenous to that state.

Landscape architects employed by the federal government are not required to be licensed.

Before licensing, a new hire will typically be called a landscape architect intern. The title is misleading, however, because interns can, depending upon their employer's requirements, perform all the duties of a licensed landscape architect. But the intern will work under the guidance of a licensed practitioner until he or she has passed the exam.

Salaries for Landscape Architects

Statistics are limited, but in 1992 salaries for entry-level bachelor's degree landscape architects started at about $20,400 per year. Those with a master's degree were able to add another $10,000 to their annual salary.

Historic Landscape Preservation

Historic landscape preservation is a field of growing interest throughout the country among managers of historic buildings and cultural and natural landscapes. The Colonial Williamsburg Foundation in Williamsburg, Virginia, is one of the largest employers of landscape architects, designers, and related groundskeeping professionals.

Kent Brinkley, Landscape Architect

Kent Brinkley is a landscape architect and garden historian at Colonial Williamsburg. He has been with the Foundation for more than ten years.

Kent talks about his job: "I wear a lot of different hats. I sit at a drawing board and I do designs for new work that's taking place. We also have a lot of gardens that were designed during the 1930s and 1940s by my predecessors, Arthur Shurcliff and Alden Hopkins. They did a lot of research and picked plants that were known and used in the eighteenth century. But in a few cases, a plant they chose, even though it was appropriate to the period, might not have been happy in a specific location because of too much sunlight or too much shade. So we try to come up with something else that would have been used but will grow better and flourish in that specific location.

"Many of these gardens are getting on in years. They're forty or fifty years old and, unlike the architecture where you just replace fabric when a board rots or you're putting a coat of paint on, plant materials do grow. They're dynamic, and when you have a garden that's mature, or overmature as many of ours happen to be, part of my charge is looking at the replacements that inevitably have to be factored in when plants or trees die out. This keeps it looking presentable to the public.

"I work closely with the director in charge of maintenance. I provide the design expertise and we talk about what is needed in a particular garden. Once a decision has been made, the maintenance staff implements the work.

"I also spend time giving slide lectures to groups and garden clubs. I give garden tours a couple of times a month to the public just to have contact with the visitors on the street.

"I'm also a garden historian. That is someone who has a background in history and has done research and is interested in the development of the historical landscape over time. I've made any number of trips to England in the last fourteen or fifteen years and have visited many country estates and gardens over there. I've looked at English landscape design, which served as the precedent for many of the designs in the eighteenth century here in the Virginia Colony. Much of my work involves looking at what was done historically in gardens. The kinds of plants that were grown, how they were laid out, the types of fencing they were using—it's all part of knowing how to recreate a period garden.

"It's a specialty someone comes to within a history curriculum. It's a young field in this country; it didn't start as a discipline until 1975. If this interests you, you would combine history courses with horticulture courses. Of course, the job market is fairly small, but it's growing. Right now most jobs are at living history museums such as Williamsburg, or Sturbridge Village and Plimoth Plantation in Massachusetts.

"When I got my job at Williamsburg I was ecstatic. This was the perfect marriage of my love of history and my concern for the environment. It's been wonderful to be able to take two major interests and combine them in a way that allows me to do both."

Kent's Background

Kent Brinkley has a B.A. in history from Mary Baldwin College in Staunton, Virginia. "I'm a dying breed—you see it less and less. But I came to landscape architecture through the back door. Just as lawyers used to be able to read the law under a licensed practitioner and then sit for the bar exam, years ago you used to be able to apprentice in a landscape architecture office under a licensed practitioner. It was an equal time commitment. In other words, when you got a five-year B.L.A. degree, you generally had to work in an office three years before you could sit for the exam. Or in lieu of that you could do eight years in an office and then take the exam. I waited ten years before I took the exam.

"I started as a draftsman and worked my way up to vice president of the firm before coming to Williamsburg."

Some Advice for Future Landscape Architects

Kent Brinkley offers the following suggestions: "People who are mechanically inclined or are curious how things fit together and work would probably find landscape architecture and drafting to their liking. There is a lot of drafting involved; you have to know how to cultivate that drawing talent. You can get a leg up on the competition that way.

"You also have to have good English skills. You need the ability to write and speak well because you're working with people every day. You might have to get up in front of a group and make a presentation to sell your designs. Some sales ability is a good thing to have; you have to market yourself, your firm, and the design, and be able to persuade people that this is the way to go. You can never waste your time by taking additional English or drawing courses.

"I always advise students that once they've graduated, they should work in several different offices and get different kinds of experiences for the first five or six years. It's not a good idea to lock yourself into any one place. Some people study landscape architecture but they don't know what facet they want to pursue. They need time to test the waters before they'll know what their niche will be.

"And it's my personal recommendation to anyone coming into the field to work for two or three years before taking the licensing exam. It's comprehensive in scope and tests you on a variety of things. You need to get some experience under your belt before you try to tackle it.

"To conclude, I can tell students I think there's a bright future in the twenty-first century. For years the architects have beat their chests and said we're the guys who are going to save the world, but they haven't. They've done some pretty wretched designs. And then the engineers said they could do it, and though they certainly design functional work, they seem to have no feeling for aesthetics. So now there's a growing awareness that landscape architects may be the people to include on the design team. We are the ones who have a broad enough range of expertise to worry about environmental concerns and other things to make the resulting projects user-friendly and earth-friendly."

Landscape Design

A landscape designer works similarly to a landscape architect but usually on residential or small commercial projects. Landscape designers are not technically certified and cannot call themselves landscape architects.

For those who do not wish to invest the number of years it takes to become a landscape architect, a career in landscape design could be the answer. To become a landscape designer you can usually do so after taking a two-year associate's degree in a landscape specialist program offered at a number of schools throughout the country.

Salaries are generally less for designers than for architects, but those who are self-employed are not as limited as those employed by a landscape architecture firm.

Foresters and Conservationists

Forests and rangelands serve a variety of needs. They supply wood products, livestock forage, minerals, and water; serve as sites for recreational activities; and provide habitats for wildlife. Foresters and conservation scientists manage, develop, use, and help protect these and other natural resources.

Although many professional foresters and forest technicians spend most of their time working outdoors during the first few years of their career, there are many who do not.

Duties outdoors include

- Measuring and grading trees

- Evaluating insect outbreaks

- Conducting land surveys

- Fighting wildfires

- Laying out road systems

- Supervising construction of trails and planting of trees

- Supervising timber harvesting

- Conducting research studies

After a few years of on-the-ground experience, foresters can advance to administrative positions and then spend less time outside. These duties include

- Planning

- Contracting

- Preparing reports

- Managing budgets

- Consulting

A professional forester has earned a four-year degree, while a forest technician normally holds an associate's degree in forest technology. Professional foresters concentrate on management skills, policy decisions, and the application of ecological concepts. Technicians generally work under a professional forester accomplishing day-to-day tasks.

Range Managers

Range managers, also called range conservationists, range ecologists, or range scientists, manage, improve, and protect rangelands to maximize their use without damaging the environment.

Soil Conservationists

Soil conservationists provide technical assistance to farmers and others concerned with the conservation of soil, water, and related natural resources. They develop programs to get the most use out of the land without damaging it.

Training for Foresters and Conservationists

In high school future foresters should concentrate on basic mathematics coursework, computer sciences, chemistry, botany, zoology, soil science, ecology, and related sciences. It is also important to have good writing and public speaking skills.

A college degree is necessary, and those with a bachelor of science degree will advance more and earn more than technicians with just an associate's degree.

The Society of American Foresters recognizes forty-six universities offering four-year degree programs and twenty-one universities offering two-year associate's degrees. For a list of these schools, contact the Society of American Foresters at the address given later in this chapter and in Appendix B.

A bachelor's degree in range management or range science is the usual minimum educational requirement for range managers; graduate degrees are required for teaching and research positions.

Very few colleges offer degrees in soil conservation. Most soil conservationists hold degrees in agronomy, general agriculture, or crop or soil science.

Finding a Job in Forestry and Conservation

The following is a partial list provided by the Society of American Foresters for those seeking employment. (For a complete list, write to the Society of American Foresters.) Send your requests for the following resources to the addresses indicated.

Be sure to ask for the most recent issue. You can also find some of these publications at your library.

Conservation Directory is updated annually and lists by states and Canadian provinces the organizations, agencies, and officials concerned with natural resource use and management. Send your request to National Wildlife Federation, 1400 16th Street, NW, Washington, DC 20036

The Ultimate Job Finders Computer Software—IBM Compatible Computers, 7215 Oak Avenue, River Forest, IL 60305.

Government Job Finders, Planning/Communications, 7215 Oak Avenue, River Forest, IL 60305.

The Professional's Job Finders, Planning/Communications, 7215 Oak Avenue, River Forest, IL 60305.

The Non-Profits' Job Finders, Planning/Communications, 7215 Oak Avenue, River Forest, IL 60305.

So You Want to be in Forestry?, The Society of American Foresters, 5400 Grosvenor Lane, Bethesda, MD 20814.

Information About Jobs Currently Available

Journal of Forestry is a monthly publication listing both positions wanted and positions available. Free to SAF members. Society of American Foresters, 5400 Grosvenor Lane, Bethesda, MD 20814.

Job Seeker lists vacancies in forestry, forest products, wildlife, fisheries, range, biology, environmental protection and education, recreation, parks, and other natural resource fields. Advertisers include timber industries, forest consultants, nurseries, federal and state agencies, universities, nature centers, and other related organizations. Write to P.O. Box 16, Warrens, WI 54666.

Environmental Career Focus is an informative newsletter including job research strategies, agency hiring plans, profiles of selected career fields, salary surveys, interviews with employers and successful job seekers, hiring trends, and a question and answer column. Four issues per year. Environmental Career Center, P.O. Box 3451, Hampton, VA 23663.

National Park Service

The National Park Service, a bureau under the U.S. Department of the Interior, administers more than 350 sites. These encompass natural and recreational areas across the country, including the Grand Canyon, Yellowstone National Park, and Lake Mead.

Because most sites are not located near major cities, serious candidates must, for the most part, be prepared to relocate. Housing may or may not be provided, depending upon the site and your position.

Park Rangers

The National Park Service hires three categories of park rangers (generally on a seasonal basis): enforcement, general and interpretation. Most health nuts concerned with the environment apply for positions in the general category.

Duties vary greatly from position to position and site to site, but rangers in the general division are usually responsible for forestry or resource management; developing and presenting programs that explain a park's historic, cultural, or archeological features; campground maintenance; firefighting; lifeguarding; law enforcement; and search and rescue.

Rangers also sit at information desks, provide visitor services, or participate in conservation or restoration projects. Entry-level employees might also collect fees, provide first aid, and operate audiovisual equipment.

Qualifications and Salaries

In determining a candidate's eligibility for employment, and at which salary level he or she would be placed, the National Park Service weighs several factors. In essence, those with the least experience or education will begin at the lowest federal government salary grade of GS-2. But the requirements for that grade are only six months of experience in related work or a high school diploma or its equivalency.

The more related work experience or education, the higher the salary level. For example, GS-4 requires eighteen months of general experience in park operations or in related fields and six months of specialized experience; one ninety-day season as a seasonal park ranger is required at the GS-3 level.

Completion of two academic years of college may be substituted for experience if the course work covered is related.

Getting Your Foot in the Door

Competition for jobs, especially at the most well-known sites, can be fierce, but the National Park Service employs a huge permanent staff, and this is supplemented tenfold by an essential seasonal work force during peak visitation periods.

The best way for a newcomer to break in is to start with seasonal employment during school breaks. With a couple of summer seasons under your belt, the doors will open more easily for permanent employment.

Because of Office of Personnel Management regulations, veterans of the U.S. Armed Forces have a decided advantage. Depending upon their experience, they may be given preference among applicants.

How to Apply

Recruitment for summer employment begins September 1 with a January 15 deadline for applications. Some sites, such as Death Valley or Everglades National Park, also have a busy winter season. The winter recruitment period is June 1 through July 15.

Applications for seasonal employment with the National Park Service can be obtained through the Office of Personnel Management or by writing to

U.S. Department of the Interior
National Park Service
Seasonal Employment Unit
P.O. Box 37127
Washington, DC 20013-7127

You may also contact one of the ten regional offices of the National Park Service. Their addresses are listed in Appendix D.

Research and Education

Only through research and the passing on of accumulated knowledge can those concerned with the environment be effective in their jobs. Keeping the earth clean and healthy is a task that could never be accomplished without worldwide cooperation. The objectives seem unobtainable, the problems insurmountable—no one person or agency could do the work alone—but dedicated professionals find ways to contribute. Each project, each research station, each talk or presentation, each person educated brings us all closer to reaching these goals.

What follows are two examples of research and education centers dedicated to improving our environment.

National Wildflower Research Center

The National Wildflower Research Center is the only national nonprofit research and educational organization committed to the preservation of native plants in planned landscapes. Founded in 1982 by Lady Bird Johnson, the Wildflower Center recently moved from its location in a former hayfield east of Austin, Texas, to a new facility with 34,000 square feet of buildings and 72,000 square feet of display gardens and educational demonstration areas. It now covers forty-two acres of Texas hill country southwest of Austin where specialists conduct educational programs and research.

The Wildflower Center is dedicated exclusively to the study, preservation, and reestablishment of native plants in public and private landscapes. The Wildflower Center strives to restore damaged habitats by sharing its knowledge and encouraging state highway departments, landscape architects and designers, developers, teachers, and backyard gardeners to use native plants.

These are some of the National Wildflower Research Center's special facilities:

- Children's garden

- Meditation garden

- Observation tower

- Three greenhouses

- Theme gardens

- Research laboratory

- Three home-comparison gardens

- Volunteer workroom

- Rainwater collection and harvesting system

- Seed silo

Staffing at the National Wildflower Research Center

At present the Wildflower Center employs the following professionals.

- Executive Director
- Editor
- Development Director
- Education Director
- Development Associate
- Horticulturist
- Two or three support staff
- Two Botanists
- Products Manager
- Landscape Manager
- Facility sales Manager
- Bookkeeper
- Public Relations and Marketing Manager
- Records/Membership Manager

Because the Wildflower Center is nonprofit and privately funded, it relies heavily on the help of more than two hundred volunteers.

Activities range from hosting fund-raisers to designing curriculum for science teachers. Volunteering at this center and others like it is an excellent way for those concerned with the environment to acquire some practical hands-on training in a number of different disciplines. For more information contact the National Wildflower Research Center, 2600 FM 973 North, Austin, TX 78725-4201.

World Forestry Center

The World Forestry Center was built in 1905 as the "Forestry Center" for the Lewis and Clark Exposition held in Portland, Oregon. Its beautiful log cabin and all of its contents were destroyed by fire in 1964. The "Western Forestry Center" was reconstructed in 1971 and renamed the World Forestry Center in 1986.

The World Forestry Center is an educational organization aiming to increase understanding of the importance of well-managed forests and their related resources. Through its publications, educational programs, exhibits, and its architecture, the Center demonstrates the benefits of conserving the forest environment.

The World Forestry Center is also dedicated to the conservation of soil, trees, wildlife, water, and other natural resources. It accomplishes its mission through scientific research, demonstrations, and the distribution of forestry information. For more information about all the varied programs and volunteering opportunities, contact the World Forestry Center, 4033 Southwest Canyon Road, Portland, OR 97221.

Environmental Engineering

It's a dirty job, but someone has to do it. Cleaning up the environment, that is. Why not you? Health nuts concerned with environmental issues can enter careers in waste management and pollution control.

What follows is a brief description of the work of a sampling of key environmental engineering jobs. They are listed in alphabetical order. For further information on each career, as well as the technician and specialist jobs that support the profession, you can write to the professional associations listed in Appendix A or refer to the *Occupational Outlook Handbook* listed in Appendix C.

Air Quality Engineers

Air quality engineers can have a variety of duties, but they are primarily problem solvers and researchers. They visit sites to investigate trouble areas, make improvement recommendations, and sometimes even enforce compliance.

To reduce pollution, they can work as consultants on new construction projects or design new pollution-reducing devices or procedures.

Civil Engineers

Civil engineering is the oldest branch of engineering. Civil engineers design and supervise the construction of roads, airports, tunnels, bridges, buildings, and water supply and sewage systems.

Specialties within civil engineering are water resource, environmental, construction, transportation, structural, and geotechnical engineering.

Civil engineers usually work near major industrial and commercial centers, often at construction sites. Some projects are located in remote areas or foreign countries.

They function as supervisors, administrators, designers, researchers, or teachers.

Oil Pollution Control Engineers

Wherever there is oil, there is the potential for an oil spill. Oil pollution control engineers try to prevent spills, but if the worst has already happened, they become involved with the cleanup process.

Oil pollution control engineers generally work under emergency conditions. They have to make split-second decisions, taking into account wind direction, tides, or water currents. They also have to coordinate the efforts of a variety of involved agencies, such as wildlife protection organizations and local fire departments.

Sanitary Engineers

Sanitary engineers work with controlling water pollution, water supply problems, and sewage disposal. Wherever there are problems, sanitary engineers investigate, taking and evaluating samples.

Sanitary engineers also make recommendations to industrial concerns, sometimes designing waste treatment programs.

Waste Management Engineers

While sanitary engineers deal with water and sewage problems, waste management engineers are concerned with solid waste management and cleanup of hazardous waste. They examine plans for disposal facilities, develop programs to make disposal more efficient, and conduct on-site inspections, often conferring with related health officials.

Training for Engineers

Engineers need to earn at least a bachelor's degree; many go on for a master's or even a doctorate. Bachelor's programs can take from four to five years to complete. Many of the specialties listed above require that the engineer be cross-trained. For example, an oil pollution control engineer would combine several disciplines such as petroleum, chemical, and civil engineering. Sanitary engineers would earn a bachelor's in civil engineering, then specialize in sanitation at the master's level.

The more areas you can specialize in within engineering, the more job situations would be open to you.

Salaries for Engineers

Engineers enjoy the distinction of having the highest starting salaries of any other bachelor's degree-level profession.

Although salaries vary branch by branch, the College Placement Council reported figures for 1992 showing that new graduates with a bachelor's degree earned an average yearly salary of $34,000. Those with a master's degree and no experience started at $39,200 a year, and those with a doctorate averaged $54,400.

Those figures are significantly higher now. What you would expect to earn would depend on the area of the country in which you lived and whether you worked in a government position or for private industry.

APPENDIX A

Professional Associations

F or more information about any of the careers highlighted throughout this book, and many others, write to the appropriate professional associations listed below. Most professional associations have prepared pamphlets and information packets including up-to-date salary figures, education requirements, and job outlooks.

Associations for Healers and Caregivers

Advocates for Child Psychiatric Nursing
437 Twin Bay Drive
Pensacola, FL 32534

American College of Nurse Midwives
1522 K Street, NW, Suite 1000
Washington, DC 20005

American College of Sports Medicine (ACSM)
Member and Chapter Services Department
P.O. Box 1440
Indianapolis, IN 46206

American Nurses Association
Library Information Center
600 Maryland Avenue, SW, Suite 100 West
Washington, DC 20024-2571

American Psychological Association
750 First Street, NE
Washington, DC 20002-4242

Association of Women's Health, Obstetric, and Neonatal Nurses
409 12th Street, SW, Suite 300
Washington, DC 20024

152

National Alliance of Nurse Practitioners
325 Pennsylvania Avenue, SE
Washington, DC 20003-1100

National Association of Orthopedic Nurses (NAON)
Box 56
East Holly Avenue
Pitman, NJ 08071

Orthopedic Certification Board (ONCB)
Box 56
East Holly Avenue
Pitman, NJ 08071

Society for Education and Research in Psychiatric–Mental Health Nursing
437 Twin Bay Drive
Pensacola, FL 32534

Associations for Healing with Plants

HERBALISM

Alternative Medicine Association
7909 Southeast Stark Street
Portland, OR 97215

American Herbalist Guild
Box 1683
Soquel, CA 95073
  Publishes a directory that lists a variety of training programs.

Flower Essence Society
P.O. Box 459
Nevada City, CA 95959

Herb Research Foundation
1007 Pearl Street, #200
Boulder, CO 80302

HORTICULTURAL THERAPY

American Horticultural Therapy Association
362A Christopher Avenue
Gaithersburg, MD 20879

Friends of Horticultural Therapy
362A Christopher Avenue
Gaithersburg, MD 20879

Associations for "Let's Get Physical" Careers

American Association for Leisure and Recreation (AALR)
1900 Association Drive
Reston, VA 22091
  The AALR publishes information sheets on twenty-five different
  careers in parks and recreation.

American Camping Association
5000 State Road 67 North
Martinsville, IN 46151
  For information on careers in camping and summer counselor opportunities.

American College of Sports Medicine (ACSM)
Member and Chapter Services Department
P.O. Box 1440
Indianapolis, IN 46206
  Provides certification for personal trainers.

American Council on Exercise (ACE)
P.O. Box 910449
San Diego, CA 92191
  Provides certification for personal trainers.

American Occupational Therapy Association
P.O. Box 1725
1383 Piccard Drive
Rockville, MD 20849-1725

American Physical Therapy Association
1111 North Fairfax Street
Alexandria, VA 22314

American Therapeutic Recreation Association
C.O. Associated Management Systems
P.O. Box 15215
Hattiesburg, MS 39402-5215

Cruise Line International Association
500 Fifth Avenue, Suite 1407
New York, NY 10110

International Physical Fitness Association
415 West Court Street
Flint, MI 48503

National Council for Therapeutic Recreation Certification
P.O. Box 479
Thiells, NY 10984-0479

National Recreation and Park Association
Division of Professional Services
2775 South Quincy Street, Suite 300
Arlington, VA 22206
   Provides information on careers and academic programs in recreation.

National Therapeutic Recreation Society
2775 South Quincy Street, Suite 300
Arlington, VA 22206-2204

YMCA of the USA
101 North Wacker Drive
Chicago, IL 60606

Associations for Careers with Food

For general information about farm occupations, opportunities, and 4–H activities, contact your local Cooperative Extension Service (highlighted in Chapter Five.)

   The following sources can also provide information about farming and agricultural occupations:

American Dietetic Association
216 West Jackson Boulevard
Chicago, IL 60606-6995

American Farm Bureau Federation
225 Touhy Avenue
Park Ridge, IL 60068

American Farmland Trust
1920 N Street, NW, Suite 400
Washington, DC 20036

American Society of Agronomy
677 South Segoe Road
Madison, WI 53711

American Society of Farm Managers and Rural Appraisers
950 South Cherry Street, Suite 106
Denver, CO 80222

Cooperative Extension Service
National Office
USDA/Extension Service
14th Street and Independence Avenue
Washington, DC 20250

Crop Society of America
677 South Segoe Road
Madison, WI 53711

Food and Agricultural Careers for Tomorrow
Purdue University
127 Agricultural Administration Building
West Lafayette, IN 47907

Institute for Alternative Agriculture
9200 Edmonton Road, Suite 117
Greenbelt, MD 20770

Institute for Food Technologists
221 North LaSalle Street, Suite 300
Chicago, IL 60601

National Association of State Departments of Agriculture
1616 H Street, NW
Washington, DC 20006

National Farmers Union
Denver, CO 80251

National Future Farmers of America Organization
P.O. Box 15160
National FFA Center
Alexandria, VA 22309

North American Farm Alliance
P.O. Box 2502
Ames, IA 50010

Northeast Organic Farming Association (NOFA)
P.O. Box 21
South Butler, NY 13154

Associations for the Health Beat

American Booksellers Association (ABA)
828 South Broadway
Tarrytown, NY 10591

American Newspaper Publishers Association Foundation
The Newspaper Center
Box 17407
Dulles International Airport
Washington, DC 20041
   The American Newspaper Publishers Association Foundation has
   career information including pamphlets titled *Newspapers: What's In It
   For Me?* and *Facts about Newspapers*.

American Society of Journalists and Authors
1501 Broadway
New York, NY 10036

American Society of Magazine Editors
575 Lexington Avenue
New York, NY 10022
   The American Society of Magazine Editors has information on college
   internships.

American Society of Media Photographers
853 Broadway
New York, NY 10003

Association of Authors Representatives (AAR)
10 Astor Place, Third Floor
New York, NY 10003

The Dow Jones Newspaper Fund
P.O. Box 300
Princeton, NJ 08543-0300
    The Dow Jones Newspaper Fund offers summer reporting and editing
    internships.

National Newspaper Association
1627 K Street, NW, Suite 400
Washington, DC 20006
    A pamphlet titled A Career in Newspapers can be obtained from the
    National Newspaper Association.

National Press Photographers Association
3200 Cloasdaile Drive, Suite 306
Durham, NC 27705
    The NPPA is an organization that can help in the job hunt. It runs a
    Job Information Bank and has regional and national divisions for
    professionals, students, and minorities.

Associations for Healing the Environment

American Chemical Society
Education Division
1155 16th Street, NW
Washington, DC 20036

American Clean Water Project
107 Spyglass Lane
Fayetteville, NY 13066

American Forestry Association
P.O. Box 2000
Washington, DC 20013

American Landscape Horticulture Association
2509 East Thousand Oaks Boulevard, Suite 109
Westlake Village, CA 91362

American Planning Association
1776 Massachusetts Avenue, NW
Washington, DC 20036

American Society of Civil Engineers
345 East 47th Street
New York, NY 10017

American Society of Landscape Architects
4401 Connecticut Avenue, NW, Fifth floor
Washington, D.C. 20008-2302

American Water Resources Association
5410 Grosvenor Lane, Suite 220
Bethesda, MD 20814

Association of State and Interstate Water Pollution Control Administration
444 North Capitol Street, NW, Suite 330
Washington, DC 20002

Bureau of Land Management
U.S. Department of the Interior
Room 3619
1849 C Street, NW
Washington, DC 20240

Colonial Williamsburg
Employment Office
P.O. Box 1776
Williamsburg, VA 23187

Council of Landscape Architectural Registration Boards
12700 Fair Lakes Circle, Suite 110
Fairfax, VA 22033

Earth Work Student Conservation Association
Box 550
Charlestown, NH 03603

JETS-Guidance
1420 King Street, Suite 405
Alexandria, VA 22314
   A clearinghouse geared toward high school students for information on
   engineering professions. Send a #10 self-addressed, stamped envelope.

National Park Service
U.S. Department of the Interior
P.O. Box 37127
Washington, DC 20013-7127
    See Appendix D for the addresses of regional offices.

National Wildflower Research Center
2600 F.M. 973 North
Austin, TX 78725-4201

National Wildlife Federation
1400 16th Street, NW
Washington, DC 20036

Society of American Foresters
5400 Grosvenor Lane
Bethesda, MD 20814

Soil Conservation Service
14th Street and Independence Avenue, SW
Washington, DC 20013

U.S. Environmental Protection Agency
Personnel Management Division (PM-212)
Washington, DC 20460

U.S. Forest Service
U.S. Department of Agriculture
14th Street and Independence Avenue, SW
Washington, DC 20250

Water Pollution Control Federation
601 Wythe Street
Alexandria, VA 22314

World Forestry Center
4033 Southwest Canyon Road
Portland, OR 97221

Selected Training Programs

Forestry

The Society of American Foresters recognizes forty-six universities offering four-year degree programs and twenty-one universities offering two-year associate's degrees. For a complete list write to

Society of American Foresters
5400 Grosvenor Lane
Bethesda, MD 20814

Herbalism

Directory of Herbal Training Programs. American Herbalist Guild, P.O. Box 1683, Soquel, CA 95073.

Horticultural Therapy Training Programs

Cleveland Botanical Garden
11030 East Boulevard
Cleveland, OH 44106
    (Six-month internship program)

Edmonds Community College
20000 68th Avenue West
Lynnwood, WA 98036
    (Two-year program in horticultural therapy)

Kansas State University
Department of Horticulture, Forestry and Recreation Resources
Throckmorton Hall
Manhattan, KS 66506
    (B.S. and M.S. programs in horticultural therapy)

Kansas State University
Office of Distance Learning
Division of Continuing Education
226 College Court Building
Manhattan, KS 66506-6007
(Short-term correspondence course)

Herbert H. Lehamn College
The City University of New York
250 Bedford Park Boulevard
West Bronx, NY 10468
(B.S. in horticulture (in cooperation with the New York Botanical Garden) with options in horticultural therapy)

Massachusetts Bay Community College
Wellesley, MA 02181
(Horticultural therapy electives)

The New York Botanical Garden
200th Street and Southern Boulevard
Bronx, NY 10458-5126
(Certificate program—179 hours/0.5 points toward AHTA professional registration)

Rockland Community College
Suffern, NY 10901
(Horticultural therapy electives)

Temple University
Department of Landscape Architecture and Horticulture
Ambler, PA 19002
(Horticultural therapy electives)

Tennessee Technological University
School of Agriculture
Box 5034
Cookerville, TN 38505
(Horticultural therapy electives)

Texas A & M University
Department of Horticulture
College Station, TX 77843-2133
(B.S. in horticulture with options in horticultural therapy)

Tulsa Junior College
Northeast Campus
Department of Science and Engineering
3727 East Apache
Tulsa, OK 74115
    (Horticultural therapy electives)

University of Massachusetts
Department of Plant and Soil Science
Durfee Conservatory, French Hall
Amherst, MA 01002
    (Horticultural therapy electives)

University of Rhode Island
Department of Plant Science
Kingston, RI 02881
    (B.S. in horticulture with options in horticultural therapy)

Virginia Polytechnic Institute and State University
Department of Horticulture
Blacksburg, VA 24061
    (Horticultural therapy electives)

APPENDIX C

Further Reading

Careers for Nature Lovers, by Louise Miller, NTC Publishing,
   Lincolnwood, IL.
Careers for Shutterbugs, by Cheryl McLean, NTC Publishing,
   Lincolnwood, IL.
Careers for Writers, by Bob Bly, NTC Publishing, Lincolnwood, IL.
Guide to Literary Agents and Art/Photo Reps, an annual from Writer's
   Digest Books, Cincinnati, OH.
How To Get A Job with a Cruise Line, by Mary Fallon Miller, Ticket to
   Adventure Publishing, P.O. Box 41005, St. Petersburg, FL 33743-1005.
   Includes descriptions of all the various jobs, an inside look at the
   different cruise lines, interviews with cruise personnel and valuable tips
   on how to go about getting a job.
How to Write a Book Proposal, by Michael Larsen, Writer's Digest Books,
   Cincinnati, OH, 1985.
How to Write Irresistible Query Letters, by Lisa Collier Cool, Writer's
   Digest Books, Cincinnati, OH, 1987.
Moosewood Restaurant Cooks at Home, by the Moosewood Collective,
   Simon & Schuster, 1994.
Moosewood Restaurant Kitchen Garden, by David Hirsch, Simon and
   Schuster, 1992.
New Recipes From Moosewood Restaurant, by the Moosewood Collective,
   Ten Speed Press, 1987.
Occupational Outlook Handbook, an annual from the Bureau of Labor
   Statistics, Superintendent of Documents, U.S. Government Printing
   Office, Washington, DC.
Opportunities in Forestry Careers, by Christopher M. Wille, NTC Publish-
   ing, Lincolnwood, IL.
Photographer's Market, an annual from Writer's Digest Books, Cincinnati,
   OH. A comprehensive listing of more than 2,500 United States and
   international buyers of free-lance photographs. Each listing gives the
   names and addresses of the buyers, how to submit your photos, what
   kind of photos they buy, pay rates, and tips on how to break in.
"Recommended Reading List," American Herbalist Guild, P.O. Box 1683,
   Soquel, CA 95073.
Sundays At Moosewood Restaurant, by the Moosewood Collective, Simon
   & Schuster, 1990.
Writer's Market, an annual from Writer's Digest Books, Cincinnati, OH.

National Park Service Regional Offices

Alaska Region
National Park Service
2525 Gambell Street
Anchorage, AK 99503

Pacific Northwest Region
National Park Service
83 South King Street, #212
Seattle, WA 98104

Western Region
National Park Service
600 Harrison Street, #600
San Francisco, CA 94107

Rocky Mountain Region
National Park Service
P.O. Box 25287
Denver, CO 80225

Southwest Region
National Park Service
P.O. Box 728
Santa Fe, NM 87501

Midwest Region
National Park Service
1709 Jackson Street
Omaha, NE 68102

Southeast Region
National Park Service
Richard B. Russell Federal Bldg
75 Spring Street, SW
Atlanta, GA 30303

Mid-Atlantic Region
National Park Service
143 South Third Street
Philadelphia, PA 19106

National Capital Region
National Park Service
1100 Ohio Drive, SW
Washington, DC 20242

North Atlantic Region
National Park Service
15 State Street
Boston, MA 02109

VGM CAREER BOOKS

CAREER DIRECTORIES
Careers Encyclopedia
Dictionary of Occupational Titles
Occupational Outlook Handbook

CAREERS FOR
Animal Lovers
Bookworms
Caring People
Computer Buffs
Crafty People
Culture Lovers
Environmental Types
Fashion Plates
Film Buffs
Foreign Language Aficionados
Good Samaritans
Gourmets
Health Nuts
History Buffs
Kids at Heart
Nature Lovers
Night Owls
Number Crunchers
Plant Lovers
Shutterbugs
Sports Nuts
Travel Buffs
Writers

CAREERS IN
Accounting; Advertising; Business;
Child Care; Communications;
Computers; Education;
Engineering;
the Environment; Finance;
Government; Health Care; High
Tech; International Business;
Journalism; Law; Marketing;
Medicine; Science; Social &
Rehabilitation Services

CAREER PLANNING
Beating Job Burnout
Beginning Entrepreneur
Career Planning & Development for
College Students &
Recent Graduates
Career Change
Careers Checklists
College and Career Success for
Students with Learning Disabilities
Complete Guide to Career Etiquette
Cover Letters They Don't Forget
Dr. Job's Complete Career Guide
Executive Job Search Strategies

Guide to Basic Cover Letter
Writing
Guide to Basic Résumé Writing
Guide to Internet Job Searching
Guide to Temporary Employment
Job Interviewing for College
Students
Joyce Lain Kennedy's Career Book
Out of Uniform
Slam Dunk Résumés
The Parent's Crash Course in
Career Planning: Helping Your
College Student Succeed

CAREER PORTRAITS
Animals; Cars; Computers;
Electronics; Fashion;
Firefighting; Music; Nursing;
Sports; Teaching; Travel; Writing

GREAT JOBS FOR
Business Majors
Communications Majors
Engineering Majors
English Majors
Foreign Language Majors
History Majors
Psychology Majors

HOW TO
Apply to American Colleges and
Universities
Approach an Advertising Agency and
Walk Away with the Job You Want
Be a Super Sitter
Bounce Back Quickly After
Losing Your Job
Change Your Career
Choose the Right Career
Cómo escribir un currículum vitae
en inglés que tenga éxito
Find Your New Career Upon
Retirement
Get & Keep Your First Job
Get Hired Today
Get into the Right Business School
Get into the Right Law School
Get into the Right Medical School
Get People to Do Things Your Way
Have a Winning Job Interview
Hit the Ground Running in Your
New Job
Hold It All Together When You've
Lost Your Job
Improve Your Study Skills
Jumpstart a Stalled Career

Land a Better Job
Launch Your Career in TV News
Make the Right Career Moves
Market Your College Degree
Move from College into a
Secure Job
Negotiate the Raise You Deserve
Prepare Your Curriculum Vitae
Prepare for College
Run Your Own Home Business
Succeed in Advertising When all
You Have Is Talent
Succeed in College
Succeed in High School
Take Charge of Your Child's Early
Education
Write a Winning Résumé
Write Successful Cover Letters
Write Term Papers & Reports
Write Your College Application Essay

MADE EASY
Cover Letters
Getting a Raise
Job Hunting
Job Interviews
Résumés

OPPORTUNITIES IN
This extensive series provides
detailed information on nearly 150
individual career fields.

RÉSUMÉS FOR
Advertising Careers
Architecture and Related Careers
Banking and Financial Careers
Business Management Careers
College Students &
Recent Graduates
Communications Careers
Education Careers
Engineering Careers
Environmental Careers
Ex-Military Personnel
50+ Job Hunters
Government Careers
Health and Medical Careers
High School Graduates
High Tech Careers
Law Careers
Midcareer Job Changes
Re-Entering the Job Market
Sales and Marketing Careers
Scientific and Technical Careers
Social Service Careers
The First-Time Job Hunter

 VGM Career Horizons
a division of *NTC Publishing Group*
4255 West Touhy Avenue
Lincolnwood, Illinois 60646–1975

Date Due
